# Gregory Tyree

# Helping Your Church Discover Its Next Pastor

## A Manual for Pastoral Search Committees

FOCUS FORWARD
PUBLISHING

Copyright © 2004, 2006, 2013 Gregory Tyree
All rights reserved
ISBN 978-1482333459

## ALSO BY GREGORY TYREE

*My Own Life Focus*

*30 Days to a Better Marriage*

*How to Lead Someone to Christ*

*God Can Turn Your Church Around*

*The Master's Peace (Handling Church Conflict)*

FOCUS FORWARD
PUBLISHING

## Table of Contents

## EDITOR'S NOTE

This manual was originally compiled and edited while I was pastoring in New Jersey and serving as the Associate Regional Director for the Mid-Atlantic Conservative Baptist Association (MACBA), now called Mission-Atlantic. I have been pastoring GracePointe Baptist Church in Madison Heights, VA, since 2005, meaning my pastoral experience includes pastoring four churches over 24 years.

Much of this book consists of excerpts and adaptations of *Here's Help: Guidelines for Seeking a Pastor*, by Rev. Burton C. Murdock, and later revised by Dr. R. Peter Mason (1996). They are used with permission. An edited version of Murdock's work can be found at the CBNorheast website. I have also gleaned considerable insight from *Procedures in Calling a Pastor* by Emmett V. Johnson (1974). This work is out-of-print, no copyright was discernible, and the author was unreachable, but I am assuming he would want his insight to help others almost forty years after he composed them. Many thanks are in order for these invaluable contributions to the cause of Christ.

Otherwise, the rest of the material in this manual is from my own experience in several congregations in the Eastern United States, as well as my former role as an executive leader of the Mid-Atlantic Conservative Baptist Association. Thus, the insight and wisdom in this book are a compilation of the minds and hearts of many people. It is my prayer that many of God's people will benefit from this resource.

Proceeds from the sales of this book are used entirely to provide materials to bi-vocational and small-church pastors.

# PREFACE

This book is about the pastoral *discovery* process. Some call it the pastoral *search* process, but I prefer the word *discovery*, because God already has a man for your church; you just need to *discover* who he is! The discovery of America, the discovery of penicillin, the discovery of the Dead Sea scrolls; these all happened by "accident," but God knew about these all along. He also knows who your next pastor is, and has already prepared him for your church! Now that's exciting!

This proactive approach is intended to be encouraging, insightful, and *intentional*! The pastoral discovery process is an exciting task, but it is not an easy endeavor. As you embark on this adventure with God, be prepared to *work*! And be prepared for difficulties. Some years ago Dr. Peter Mason wrote:

> *Dr. Leith Anderson in his book,* A Church for the 21st Century *(1994), warns, "A clergy dearth is coming." He observes that this shortage is "predictable just in terms of those approaching retirement and the greatly reduced number of ministerial candidates."*

> *There are additional reasons for the scarcity of competent pastors. In many churches the minister compensation is not economically feasible for raising a family. There are unrealistic expectations on the pastor and his family leading to burnout. There is a general disrespect for pastoral leadership. Many capable pastors are no longer in the ministry and spiritually sensitive young people avoid that vocation when they do not see the pastor valued in their local church.*

> *Dr. Anderson concludes, "All these factors point to a coming shortage. There will be a switch from the recent buyer's market to a seller's market. Churches will have a much more difficult time finding pastors, will probably expend more time and energy to find effective pastors, and will work much harder to retain those they have."*

*A wise church family will humbly and prayerfully seek a new pastor, commit themselves to a supportive relationship with him, and offer as generous compensation as they are able. In spite of the trends, the Spirit of God continues to graciously gift His Church with capable pastoral leadership.*

*Jesus said to his disciples, "The harvest is plentiful but the workers are few. Ask the Lord of the harvest, therefore, to send out workers into his harvest field" (Matthew 9:37-38). Our communities are part of the harvest field!*

Fortunately, the trend may have changed since my colleague penned these prophetic words, and maybe they have changed because pastors like Dr. Mason spoke out concerning the impending pastoral dearth. Churches *are* succeeding in discovering, evaluating, calling, and compensating their pastors, but only those churches that have done so *intentionally*!

In my opinion, based on almost twenty-five years of experience as a pastor of four churches in three states, as well as my past role as Associate Director of a regional church association, one of the obstacles facing churches hoping to discover a new pastor in the 21st century is *pluralism*. There are few colleges, seminaries, and leadership training institutions that prepare pastoral candidates to know what they truly believe. This may seem strange, or even astonishing to some readers, but the truth is theological pluralism is on the rise, and it doesn't seem that it will stop anytime soon.

As churches intentionally set out to discover their pastors, they will need to know "what they are looking for." What does your church believe? What hills will your church "die on"? What matters to your church? These are vital questions that must be answered if you are to discover the man *God* has for your church. God is already at work in your church, and He will not lead someone to you that is not the right fit for your church. If the fit is wrong, the process went awry somewhere along the line. I hope this book will help you succeed at discovering the man who "fits" your church.

# INTRODUCTION

The uniqueness of Baptist policy is never more apparent than when a Baptist church calls a pastor. The man who comes, comes at the call of the church through his own sense of the leading of the Holy Spirit. Baptist pastors are not placed by a Regional Director or other executive. A Regional Director may offer guidance and counsel, but ultimately it is the local church, which under God makes the choice of its own pastor.

Therefore, what is offered in these pages is to help the church do its own work. The guidelines and suggested procedures reflect Baptist usage generally accepted as ethical, sensible means to help church and pastor find God's leading in this crucial matter of calling a pastor.

Dean Omark stresses some basic principles that must be kept in mind as the church undertakes the task of calling a pastor.

1. We need to reaffirm the conviction that God has prepared a man to fill the pulpit.

2. God should be the prime mover in the process by which a pastor is obtained… God can be expected to reveal His will in a manner that facilitates the calling of the right person…God reveals His plan and expects human cooperation for its execution.

3. The church, under God, should take the initiative in seeking to fill the empty pulpit… "the place must seek the preacher…"

I like to think of this in an ironic way; the sheep are looking for (trying to discover) their shepherd. This is strange, indeed. In the corporate world, it is usually a board or an individual who places a CEO or other type of leader. In the educational world, college presidents are chosen by trustees and regents, not by the students or the faculty. But in the church, in the final analysis, the "CEO" or "president," that is, the pastor, is ultimately, under God, "chosen" by the people who the shepherd will serve.

This book will help churches "choose well." Like any resource, this book is only as good as its application. The Pastoral Discovery Team must "plan their work and work their plan." Teams with "good intentions" don't plan to fail; they fail to plan. A great plan executed with enthusiasm and precision will go far in the discovery of your next pastor. May God bless you in this holy endeavor.

*Note:* *Throughout this work, "pastor(s)" is always in the masculine gender. Likewise, the pastor's spouse is always referred to as the pastor's "wife." This is not a literary convenience, but reflects the conviction of the author that according to the New Testament, pastors are to be men. This is not meant to be a hindrance or to be divisive, but merely an honest reflection of the author's perspective and beliefs.*

# Chapter One
## Situation: The Reasons for Pastoral Vacancies

Many churches and pastoral discovery teams overlook the significance of the reason for a previous pastor's departure; the *situation* that caused the pastoral vacancy and the *situation* the pastoral vacancy places the church in. Understanding the dynamics of these reasons may help a pastoral discovery team in finding the *right* man for the job! Below is a list of ten reasons pastors leave churches, and how these reasons affect the church. You should try to identify the reason that best describes your current situation and use that information to help you in the process of discovering your new pastor!

## 1. Death

It may sound strange, or even morbid, for me to say this, but a pastoral vacancy by death is sometimes the least difficult to deal with, so far as *replacing* the pastor goes. While the death of a pastor is and should be devastating to the church emotionally, it eliminates a lot of the reasons that cause problems when it comes to replacing the pastor. Here are some issues you won't face when there is a pastoral vacancy by death:

- Why did our pastor leave us?

- Why does he want to go to another ministry instead of staying with us?

- What did we do to our pastor to make him leave us?

- Is there a group in the church who ran our pastor off?

- What could we have done to keep our pastor?

- Etc.

In most cases, it is an elderly pastor that dies. While this is accompanied by mourning, grief, and nostalgia, it usually isn't accompanied by bitterness, confusion, and anger. When a younger pastor dies, however, the church will oftentimes plummet into despair, guilt, bitterness, anger, and confusion. Whatever the circumstances surrounding the death of a pastor, the church should have an experienced minister, denominational leader, or other ministry consultant to come alongside them to help them through such a transition. The church must "deal with" the death of their pastor before seeking to replace him.

Many church consultants, denominational executives, and church health experts recommend that a church that loses its pastor by death should secure an interim pastor before seeking a permanent one. Such an interim pastor should serve a minimum of six months to a maximum of two years. The interim should be seasoned and well prepared for the dynamics that are produced by the death of a pastor. As with most interim pastors, the church should avoid considering the interim as their permanent pastor, and the interim pastor should not seek the position. This is best achieved by contract between the church and the interim pastor.

## 2. Retirement

Pastoral vacancy by retirement is one of the least disruptive ways to "lose" a pastor. While the new pastor may live in "the shadow" of a well-loved long-tenured pastor, the pastoral retirement is generally a time of affirmation, validation, and celebration of what God has done in the church through the retiring pastor. In today's church environment, it is unusual to actually see a pastor retire from a church! There is such a high level of turnover in pastors that a church that sees its pastor to retirement is more than likely a pastor-loving church. There are, however, a few concerns that need to be addressed when replacing a retiring pastor:

- Is the church truly willing to put the past behind them and not expect the new pastor to be an updated version of the old one?

- Is the retiring pastor leaving the area? If not, be prepared for some difficulties. It is rare that allowing a retired pastor to "stay on as an honored member" actually works. In most cases the retired pastor must leave. If the church is not prepared to enforce this, it isn't prepared for a new pastor. One of the determining factors is the opinion of the new pastor. Allow him to make this decision *after* you have called him, not as a *condition* of the call.

- Is the church hoping to have another long-term pastor? If so, you may want to consider candidates under the age of forty-five. This way, you may expect a pastor to stay for twenty years or more. As will be stated elsewhere in this book, however, older pastors tend to stay longer than younger ones.

- Has the church made some kind of long-term financial agreement with the retiring pastor (such as annual stipend payments for life, free housing, etc.) that may have an adverse effect on the church and incoming pastor?

- Is the pastoral candidate going to be in communication with the retiring pastor?

- Is the retiring pastor going to be involved in helping the church in discovering his successor? This is probably a healthy thing, as long as the retiree is not trying to vicariously extend or project himself into perpetuity.

In the final analysis, a church must plan for its pastor's retirement in a healthy way, and part of that is planning for his replacement. You might want to ask the retiring pastor to prepare a report for pastoral candidates that states his opinions regarding church health, areas of strengths and weaknesses, a true financial picture, staff relations and issues, community reputation and exposure, vision, mission, and strategies espoused, etc. View the pastoral discovery process as "passing the baton" of leadership from a retiring shepherd to the new shepherd.

### 3. Personal Situation

Pastors are people (you did know that, didn't you?), and as such, they can have personal problems and situations that require their move to a new ministry or out of vocational ministry. While most churches are sensitive to this fact, some congregations need a little education in this area. Some personal reasons that may cause a pastor to leave are:

- Serious and prolonged family illness (including the pastor)

- Serious illness or situation with the pastor's (or pastor's wife's) parents, etc.

- Financial devastation

- Need for more formal education

- Career transition for the pastor's wife

- Need to be near adult children or grandchildren

- Etc.

One of the problems with pastoral personal situations is that they are so open to public scrutiny and interpretation. What may be okay for someone else is often not deemed okay for the pastor. For example, if the pastor's wife has a career and is asked to transfer out of the area, you can count on the fact that the pastor will be criticized "big time" if he makes the move. Consider the fact that the pastor may depend on his wife's income, in which case the church may not be compensating adequately. Or if the pastor leaves to be near children or grandchildren consider how important family is, even to ministers! After all, the Lord can still use him in another geographic area. Serving God and being with family are not mutually incompatible.

If the pastor has sick family members or has, for whatever reason, gone through a devastating financial situation that requires that he work elsewhere, the church must adapt to such situations and move on. The key here is to not let the circumstances of an exiting pastor affect your views and treatment of a prospective pastor. Every situation must be treated on a "case by case" basis. It is wise to discuss your church's view of pastoral personal issues with a pastor *before* you call him.

## 4. A New Call

One of the most difficult things for a church is when its well-loved pastor accepts a call to another congregation. This almost always results in confusion, hurt feelings, disappointment, lost dreams, and, in some cases, anger and resentment. After all, the pastor chose someone else over his current church, didn't he? No, God did. Here are some thoughts to consider:

- God's call to ministry is permanent; the location isn't

- God often uses one ministry to prepare someone for another ministry

- A Pastor grows or changes personally, which often requires that he seek another ministry

- The pastor may sense that he is a hindrance to his current ministry and, to him, leaving is viewed as a blessing for the church he loves

- The pastor has lost his vision for his current ministry and must ethically seek another calling

There are many reasons God calls a man to another ministry. If pastoral turnover is frequent in your church, you may want to consider why pastors do not stay with you.

## 5. A New Calling

Sometimes a pastor leaves because of a new *calling*. That is, he is exiting pastoral *church* ministry altogether. There are essentially two types of *new calling*: 1) a transition into a non-congregational type of ministry (e.g. para-church, seminary, or denominational ministry, etc.); and 2) a transition into what we call "secular" work.

When a pastor leaves your church to be a seminary professor or denominational leader you might actually feel a sense of pride, knowing that your pastor has vision and competence to succeed in many ministry arenas. If he leaves and goes into secular work, however, you may want to ask yourselves, "What caused our pastor to leave vocational ministry? Is there anything that we did as a church that contributed to this decision? Are we as a church contributing to pastoral contentment or pastoral resentment?"

These and other questions must be answered before pursuing a new pastor. The best person to ask is the exiting pastor. Try to have a fair and non-confrontational exit interview with him. If there are unresolved issues, hurt feelings, antagonism, or anger issues, by all means, and for the Lord's sake, attempt to resolve these. Don't bring a new pastor into a situation in which he must deal with old, unresolved pastoral issues.

## 6. Mutually Agreed Upon Resignation

While no church would call a pastor who they do not feel is "their man" and while no pastor will accept a call to a church that he feels does not "fit him," sometimes a pastor and a church are simply not "working out." Maybe they did work well together when the relationship began, or maybe it's been an "uphill climb" since the beginning, but when the pastor and church are not "getting along" or simply do not "fit," it's time for the pastor to move on.

Praise the Lord that the pastor and church each have the wisdom to know that some good (or not-so-good) things must come to an end. No one likes to give or receive a resignation, but when it is mutually agreeable, it can be a smooth, even if difficult transition.

This does not mean, however, that both sides are mutually to blame when things do not work out. There are times when a pastor has been wronged by his church, or finds himself in a difficult church to pastor, yet desires to cause no hurt or pain for the church, so he simply "agrees" to go. There are other times when a church does not have the heart to let an ineffective or ill-suited pastor go, and are glad when he finally agrees that he should leave.

Even when a resignation is mutual, the church must still consider if it contributed in some negative way to the exit of the pastor. As mentioned in the previous points, a church who loses its pastor must determine if they are somehow overtly or covertly the culprit. Such corporate soul-searching can only be positive for the church. Again, attempt a positive and fair exit interview with the exiting pastor.

## 7. Forced Resignation

A forced resignation is when a pastor is told he must resign or forfeit some "benefits" that he will receive if he resigns willfully. Such "benefits" may include a severance package, a good reference for future employment, or an allowance for an extended stay in the parsonage, etc. In reality, the pastor is being fired, but with some grace and maybe an opportunity to "save face" and retain some dignity.

Many pastors blow it at this point. I have succeeded two pastors who did not handle their "forced resignations" well. They used the forced resignations as their opportunity to let the church know how badly "those ungodly deacons" treated them. In both cases, it merely left the church in turmoil and division.

While a church can hardly control how a pastor resigns, it can control how its actions precipitate or contribute to the termination of the pastor. Before pursuing a new pastor, deal with the issues of the forced resignation of the exiting pastor. If this is not your church's first forced termination, you may want to do some collective evaluation and try to determine if your church is dysfunctional in the way it treats its pastors. Sometimes an outside person, such as a denominational leader or respected pastor, can help you in this area. Don't move forward until you've taken care of this issue.

## 8. Termination

When a pastor refuses to leave a church voluntarily, the church board may terminate him. Worse yet, depending on your church's governance, the church may "vote him out!" If it is at all possible, never "fire" (terminate) a pastor publicly. People in secular vocations are given the courtesy of being terminated in the privacy of a manager's office (unless the manager is a real jerk). The best way to terminate a pastor, if you absolutely must, is to have one or two representatives from the elders or deacons do it, or, at the most, have the pastor come before the board only, and not the congregation.

If you have terminated your last pastor, take great heed to the advice already offered in the previous points. You may have been entirely right and justified in terminating your pastor, but if the church somehow contributed to the problem, it must deal with this before calling another pastor. As with the previous point, if you have fired more than one pastor, outside help is a must before proceeding to call another possibly vulnerable pastor.

## 9. Moral or Spiritual Failure of the Pastor

This is obviously one of the worst ways (if not *the* worst way) to lose a pastor. A pastoral moral failure can devastate the church, often to the "point of no return!" At my first church, I was the fifth pastor following the founding pastor who had a moral failure, which was in this case, a homosexual affair. A small church in an aging village does not survive this sort of thing short of a miracle. Twenty-five years had elapsed since the pastor's indiscretion, and the shame still hovered over the church like a giant shadow. But, praise the Lord, the church eventually was able to turn around and grow to a record size!

One of the most difficult things about pastoral moral failure is defining what it is; i.e. what it *includes*. It can be as private and subtle as internet pornography, or as open and stark as an outright physical indiscretion. Keep in mind, too, that moral failure is not limited to sexual sin, though sexual sin is arguably the worst kind of sin. A moral failure can be a financial debacle, a scandal of deceit, or a serious breaking of the law. It may involve drug addiction, spousal abuse, or problems related to a lack of self-control. It would behoove a church to establish guidelines of what constitutes a moral failure and the precipitating consequences *before* a moral failure happens. It is much easier to deal with such an issue without a name attached to it. If you are without a pastor because of a moral failure, here are some things to do (or not to do):

- By all means be sure that the accusation of moral failure has been substantiated and documented. There is absolutely NO room for hearsay, and no one should be dismissed simply for appearance' sake.

- Do not "black-list" the failing pastor. It is up to the Lord, not the local church, to decide if he is to ever return to pastoral ministry.

- Determine who will handle future references for the dismissed pastor, and how such references will be disclosed. Seek legal advice.

- If at all possible, allow the failing pastor to resign privately. Private sins need only to be confessed privately (such as before the board). If the failure is public, involves a large number of people, or has "leaked" to the public, deal with it publicly, but by no means beyond the absolute sphere of those affected.

- Keep everything on the up-and-up; do NOT cover things up.

- With the help of a qualified outside party, establish a plan of action regarding public relations. While you do not want to cover anything up, you do not want to handle the situation inappropriately or foolishly, either.

- Establish a healthy recovery plan for the pastor and his family; do NOT write him off.

- Be as compassionate as possible to the pastor and his family; remember that no one is without sin.

- Determine the effects of the failure on the wife and children, and seek to help in anyway the church can.

- Do NOT "pretend" that the moral failure did not happen, and do NOT minimize the severity of the failure.

- On the other hand, do not blow the failure out of proportion. Exaggerating an already shameful situation will help no one.

- Determine if the church in anyway contributed to the pastor's predisposition toward moral failure.

- Do not seek another pastor until you have properly dealt with the moral failure issue.

- Seriously consider an "intentional interim pastor" to immediately succeed the pastor. Allow the church to "heal" and really move on.

- Agree as a church NOT to be cynical about pastors in general. Do not assume that all pastors are immoral, and do not project past issues on your new pastor.

You may be interested to know that there are almost 400,000 churches in the United States. Including senior pastors and staff pastors, there are over a million pastors in the United States. Now, try to add up all of the pastoral moral failures (actual, not merely "accused") you heard about this past year. Add up all you have heard about altogether. What is the number? Is it five? Ten? Let's be really liberal with this and say that you can name twenty pastoral moral failures. Do the math. That's only .002% (2 1000ths of 1%). If there were 100 pastoral moral failures per state last year (this is hypothetical- there was most likely NOT that many moral failures), the number would have been 5000. Even with that number, the total of pastoral moral failures would only be .5% (½ of 1%) of the whole. This is not to say that pastoral moral failure is insignificant or trivial; on the contrary. It is to say that it is extremely rare. The point is that the preponderance of pastors is morally pure! Almost 100% of them are! Keep this in mind when a pastoral moral failure hits home. It is the exception, not the rule. Be open-minded and non-cynical when seeking to discover your next pastor.

## 10. Sin in the Church

A church must not make the grave mistake of ignoring its collective contribution to pastoral departures. Like pastoral moral failure, churches losing pastors over "sin in the camp" is rare, but it is not unheard of. Before you seek to discover your next pastor, determine if there is internal church sin (individual and collective) that caused the departure of your last pastor. There are some indicators of internal church sin:

- Frequent pastoral turnover.

- Constant church conflict and turmoil.

- A controlling member(s) or family (or families).

- Lack of church discipline.

- High level of pride in the church.

- Inappropriate view and/or treatment of pastoral leadership.

- Tolerance of unbiblical teachings.

- Low standard of spiritual separation.

- High level of legalism or liberalism.

- Inordinate value placed on tradition and polity.

- Frequent conflict in business meetings.

- Lack of evangelistic zeal.

- Newcomers not welcomed and assimilated.

- Complacency and laziness regarding church mission and vision.

- "Country Club" mentality is maintained.

- Etc.

If there is incessant and un-confessed sin in the church, no amount of hard work, sincerity, and effective pastoral searching will overcome the imminent failure of the church. By no means should you seek a new pastor before dealing with church sin. An interim pastor, preferably an experienced and seasoned pastoral veteran, is surely necessary, but do NOT seek a permanent pastor until church sin is purged.

## CONCLUSION

There are probably more reasons for pastoral turnover, but these ten should serve as a good primer to help you identify your *situation*. Now that you have evaluated the situation that precipitated the pastoral vacancy, as well as the situation you are in as a church, it is now time to interpret the internal climate of your church (after you "work it out" for chapter one).

## PASTORAL DISCOVERY TEAM- CHAPTER ONE- *WORK IT OUT!*

Together determine the reason for your pastoral vacancy. State it in a word or phrase: _____. Now, describe the situation in a paragraph or two:

_____
_____
_____
_____
_____

Based on your situation, state whether you should seek a permanent pastor now, or secure an interim: _____ Why?

_____
_____
_____
_____

List ten action steps that will help you begin the process of discovering your next pastor (or interim pastor), keeping in mind the circumstances of your pastoral vacancy:

1. _____

2. _____

3. _____

4. _____

5. _____

6. _____

7. _____

8. _____

9. _____

10. _____

Together, as a team, take time to thank the Lord for your previous pastor, regardless how he left, or how the church felt about him when he left. Pray for your previous pastor and his family, and pray for each other on the team.

## Chapter Two
## Interpretation: Discerning the Church's Pre-Discovery Climate

This chapter will be quite brief, but it is necessary to deal with the questions, "How healthy is our church?" and "How can our church remain in a healthy state, even before we discover our new pastor?"

There is probably no such thing as a "totally" healthy church. Think about it this way. If you can imagine the healthiest person in the world (a body-builder, athlete, personal trainer, etc), do you think there would be "nothing" wrong with him or her? There would be some blemish or some imperfection, even if trivial. As your church seeks to stay healthy or return to health, it may be better to ask, "Is my church *becoming* healthy?" Is it getting healthier? Is it *becoming* what it ought to be?

There are many theories about church health. Just about every pastor knows about Rick Warren's *Purpose Driven Church* concepts. Many know of Dan Spader's *Growing a Healthy Church* (GHC) or the work of George Barna. One of my mentors and a couple of my colleagues are participating in a very effective program called *Ministry Advantage*. It would behoove the wise leadership team to implement some form of church-growth (or church-health) measurement tool that helps them move the church toward health and gives them insight as to how their church is doing in the area of church health.

Regardless of which track you use, if any, almost all the church-health leaders and leadership institutes concur that there are eight to ten characteristics (qualities) of a healthy church. Since I use a ministry health model called *Natural Church Development*, I will use its eight characteristics of a healthy church as a guideline for you to measure your church's health, and determine your "pre-pastoral discovery climate." Most church health literature agrees that these qualities are universally seen in healthy churches. I have added a ninth quality, "Generous Stewardship".

## The Nine Qualities of a Healthy Church

### 1. Empowering Leadership

The importance of leadership is no secret to the modern church leader. The key here, however, is *empowering* leadership. Empowered leaders understand the Ephesians Four Principle: the pastor's role is to "equip the saints to do the work of the ministry". Healthy churches' leaders do not only *do* ministry, they empower others to do it! They:

- Lead by example

- Train the people for ministry

- Release the people for ministry

- Provide the resources for ministry

- Encourage those who minister

- Etc.

Before you begin to discover your next pastor, determine if your church has empowering leadership. This is vital to the success of the next pastor. The quality of your church's leadership will, to a great extent, determine the level of success for your new pastor.

### 2. Gift-Oriented Ministry

One cannot overemphasize the importance of Spiritual Gifts discovery and development. The healthy church strives to *educate* people to know their Spiritual Gifts and *empower* them to use them! It is an irrefutable fact: people are more effective and content when working within their areas of giftedness.

The spiritual gift-mix of your congregation greatly affects your need for a pastor. If your church is weak in evangelism, you may want to seek a pastor who is a gifted teacher of evangelism. If your church is weak in doctrine, you may want to call a gifted expositor. If your church is strong in worship, you may want to seek a pastor who knows how to emphasize this strength for further congregational growth and maturity. Understanding gift-oriented ministry can help you in discovering your next pastor. See my book, *Discovering Your Spiritual Gifts*, available at Amazon.com or as a free PDF download at www.GregoryKTyree.com.

## 3. Passionate Spirituality

The obvious qualifying word here is *passionate*. Healthy churches are not filled with self-righteous people or indifferent people; they are filled with spiritually impassioned people. Spiritually passionate people have a healthy "obsession" with God and for ministry.

Ask yourself this question: When our next pastor arrives, what will he think about our level of passion? Will he see the church as lethargic? Will our congregation seem indifferent? Will he see a congregation that is really "on fire" for God? If you sense that your congregation is indifferent or merely maintaining the status quo, perhaps a dynamic, driven and "cheerleading" type of pastor is called for. If your church is a dynamic and energetic flock, you will want to avoid a "stick in the mud" pastor. You get the picture.

## 4. Functional Structures

Many churches have growth-deterring "structures". In *Natural Church Development*, "structures" refers to the parliamentary, procedural, and policy paradigms in place. This includes church constitutions, bylaws, and policy manuals, as well as the unwritten rules and regulations of the church. Healthy churches eliminate as many of the "hoops to jump through" as possible. While unhealthy churches focus on form, healthy churches focus on function. There is a need for form, but it must be Biblical, practical, and promote church health.

The Pastoral Discovery Team needs to challenge the church to ask itself the following questions: Are there structures in place in our church that predispose us to the status quo? Will our next pastor find our protocols to be growth-friendly or growth-deterrents? Is there anything about our constitution or bylaws we should change before our new pastor arrives? And the most important question, are we willing to allow the next pastor to lead us in such changes of structure? Your answers to these questions are pertinent to the success of your next pastor (and thus your church!).

## 5. Inspiring Worship Services

Every church has worship "services". Healthy churches have *inspiring* worship services! This has nothing to do with the style (form) of worship, but the effect (function) of worship. Healthy churches *experience* God on a regular basis.

Your church's worship style and its attitude toward it will have an effect on the next pastor (just as it did on the previous pastor). If your church needs to be more effective at reaching the younger generation, it may need to transition to (or maintain) a dynamic contemporary worship style. Your new pastor must be able to lead in this. If your congregation is determined to retain a traditional form of worship, and is not likely to compromise in this area, you will want pastoral candidates to know this. Never imply that your church will change in an area that it will most likely not.

Today, this is one of the key areas of conflict in churches. This is called "the worship wars." While it is not within the scope of this book to defend one philosophy of worship over another, suffice it to say that the pastor's philosophy of worship must be compatible with the congregation's. While there are exceptions, when it comes to worship wars between a pastor and a church, the church usually wins. If you desire to keep a pastor long-term, you must deal with this issue *before* you call him. The simplest way to do this is to "ask."

## 6. Holistic Small Groups

Healthy churches have a considerable number of its people participating in holistic small groups. These groups provide discipleship, accountability, companionship, community, and education. While many churches have lots of small groups, healthy churches have *holistic* small groups. These groups can come in the form of something as traditional as a Sunday School Class, or they may be meetings geographically located in homes or based on the life-stages of the people.

If your church has a well-established and effective small group program, you will want to call a pastor who supports this type of ministry. If you are weak in this area, but desire to improve, you may want to consider a pastor who is gifted and passionate about holistic small groups. Discuss this in the interview process.

## 7. Need-Oriented Evangelism

Healthy churches do not see the Social-Gospel/Salvation-Gospel evangelism dichotomy as an either/or issue; they see it as a both/and issue. In other words, healthy churches see needs and meet them so that they might share the Gospel with the lost in their community and world. Healthy churches know their primary activity apart from worshipping God is reaching the lost. This urgency keeps the healthy church from getting bogged down with trivia and nonsense.

Therefore, healthy churches will want to call a pastor who places a high priority on reaching the lost. When interviewing a candidate, ask him about his philosophy of preaching evangelistically. Determine his ideas about programs, ministries, staff development, and strategic planning that help facilitate evangelism. Enquire about his passion (or lack thereof) for missions and world evangelism. A rule of thumb is if the candidate does not currently have a passion for evangelism, he will not have such a passion just because you want him to.

If your church neither is nor desires to become an evangelistic church, this should be conveyed to any serious candidate. Fewer things frustrate an evangelistic pastor more than the resistance of a non-evangelistic church, and fewer things frustrate an evangelistic church more than a non-evangelistic pastor. The reverse of these situations is true, as well.

## 8. Loving Relationships

Healthy churches are relational churches. In healthy churches people matter more than policies, facilities, budgets, programs, tradition, etc. Loving relationships are based on a common love for Christ. Healthy churches know that the church is people, and they behave that way.

It is imperative that the Pastoral Discovery Team discerns the personable-ness (or lack thereof) of the candidate. Because of the importance of relationships in today's society, churches generally want relational pastors. This is easily determined by interacting with the candidate and by visiting his current church (if that is possible). It is much more difficult, however, to determine if a pastor is personable than if he is a good preacher. Insight from a denominational executive or some other specialist who knows the candidate shall be invaluable at this juncture.

## 9. Generous Stewardship

Finally, healthy churches are generous churches. Whether we like it or not, most ministries, at least corporate ministry, cost money. Facilities, programs, staffing, and a plethora of other resources require finances. Growing, healthy churches, though not necessarily "rich," usually have the resources to "do ministry".

A perceptive candidate will want to know about the church's finances, and a perceptive church will want to know how a candidate views church finances. What is his view on tithing? How does he do fundraising? What is his attitude toward debt? All these questions and more must be answered to insure that the new pastor and church are on the same table regarding finances.

The Pastoral Discover Team should, with the church board's help (and the congregation in general), determine the relative health of the church in these nine areas, as well as other areas it may deem important. The team can do an informal survey by using the form on the next page.

## NINE QUALITIES OF A HEALTHY CHURCH
### (Based on Natural Church Development™

As objectively as possible, rate your church in the following nine areas ("0" meaning "we really stink in this area" and "10" meaning that "we are doing exceptionally well in this area").

**Empowering Leadership**

1    2    3    4    5    6    7    8    9    10

**Gift-Oriented Ministry**

1    2    3    4    5    6    7    8    9    10

**Passionate Spirituality**

1    2    3    4    5    6    7    8    9    10

**Functional Structures**

1    2    3    4    5    6    7    8    9    10

**Inspiring Worship Service**

1    2    3    4    5    6    7    8    9    10

**Holistic Small Groups**

1    2    3    4    5    6    7    8    9    10

**Need-Oriented Evangelism**

1    2    3    4    5    6    7    8    9    10

**Loving Relationships**

1    2    3    4    5    6    7    8    9    10

**Generous Stewardship**

1    2    3    4    5    6    7    8    9    10

With your leadership team, develop a strategy to improve each area of church health, paying especially close attention to the minimum factor (weakest area). Seriously consider contacting Natural Church Development for more information.

**PASTORAL DISCOVERY TEAM- CHAPTER TWO *WORK IT OUT!***

Together determine the relative health of your church. State it in a word or phrase: _____. Now, describe your church's health in a paragraph or two:

_____

_____

_____

_____

_____

Based on your church's health, what are some things that should be done before seeking a new pastor?

_____

_____

_____

_____

_____

Listing one (1) major point for each of the nine healthy characteristics, make a list of concerns, thoughts, or insights that will help you in this process, as well as help any candidates considering your church. Add a tenth characteristic if necessary.

1. _____

2. _____

3. _____

4. _____

5. _____

6. _____

7. _____

8. _____

9. _____

10. _____

Together, as a team, take time to thank the Lord for your church, regardless of its health. Pray for your church, specifically regarding the nine characteristics of a healthy church. Determine to discover a pastor who is passionate about all of these areas of ministry.

# Chapter Three
## Anticipation: The Stages of the Pastoral Discovery Process

A church that finds itself without a pastor usually begins a journey through as many as eight stages of change and progression. Each stage is normal and should be accepted as part of the process of moving from what was to what will be. This time of transition can be an opportunity for spiritual growth within the church family.

Most resources on pastoral discovery maintain that a typical church will average between six months to a year before calling its next pastor. While this seems like an "eternity" to a church without a shepherd, this time is necessary to assure that the church has gone through the various stages of acceptance and adjustment, as well as taking the proper amount of time (i.e. not rushing in) to discover its new pastor.

### Stage One: Alarm

While some churches can anticipate a pastoral vacancy (i.e. approaching retirement, pastoral unhappiness, etc.), most congregations will be "shocked" (alarmed) when their pastor resigns (or is asked to leave). This period of alarm is important to understand. When at all possible, the following are some steps to consider.

- Always be upfront as to why the pastor has resigned or is leaving

- Try not to "blame" one side or the other; this only contributes to congregational disunity

- Seriously deal with the issues that precipitated the vacancy

- When appropriate, affirm the leaving pastor, and give a proper send-off

- Allow for questions and concerns to be voiced openly

- Compose a well-written and optimistic (even though realistic) letter that is sent to all members, helping them to understand what has happened and what they can expect to happen in the near future

- Establish absolute unity among the leaders (elders, deacons, etc.) of the church

- Assure the congregation that God is in control, and that He already knows who the next pastor will be!

- It is imperative that any pastoral staff handle this first stage well. Pastoral staff can be key in getting the church through this initial stage

- Unless otherwise provided for, no pastoral staff should seek to fill, or be allowed to aspire to, the senior pastoral vacancy

- Communicate, communicate, communicate!

There may be other steps you will want to consider, but the important thing is to handle this first stage well. Much of what happens later depends on it.

**Stage Two: Anxiety**

The termination of a pastor's ministry raises some natural questions such as: Why did our pastor choose to leave our church? What changes do we need to make in our lives? Who will replace our pastor? Who will perform all the services he did? How can we help serve the church family in this time of transition? Where do we turn for help in the preaching responsibilities? Will people lose interest while we are without a pastor?

All the anxieties of a church family, like all the anxieties of an individual, need to be committed to the Lord. He is the Head of the Body and cares for it. "Do not be anxious about anything," Paul admonished, "but in everything, by prayer and petition, with thanksgiving, present your requests to God" (Philippians 4:6). Some churches challenge their people to seasons of corporate prayer and fasting concerning the needs of the church and the search for a new pastor. When you do this, God's transcending peace exceeds all your questions and concerns.

## Stage Three: Anger or Anguish

Depending on the circumstances regarding the pastoral vacancy, your church may experience anger or anguish (or both) after the fact of the pastoral vacancy "sinks in." There are many reasons for this. The people may feel angry at the pastor for "leaving them," or they may feel angry at some person or group of persons for "running him off." They may feel anguish because of their great love for the previous pastor, or from fear as to what will happen during the interim. Regardless of the reasons, anger and anguish can often be expected and must be dealt with. Here are a few suggestions.

- Seek reconciliation between the leaving pastor and any parties that may have something against him (or he against them)

- Attempt to bring unity between any dissenting or disagreeing factions within the congregation

- Teach the congregation that it is God's business where He sends a pastor; they should not be angry with the leaving pastor

- If the exiting pastor precipitated the reasons for the anger, he may want to somehow "apologize" to the church, or otherwise seek reconciliation

- If the church has somehow "mistreated" the pastor, or otherwise committed some kind of corporate sin, it must deal with this, including seeking forgiveness and reconciliation, both with God and the exiting pastor.

Take a look at chapter one (regarding the reasons for pastoral vacancies) to see if there is any insight to be gleaned at this juncture of the process. Needless to say, the entire search process will be difficult if this stage is not handled well. Even if you call a new pastor, problems are sure to arise later if things are not done correctly here.

## Stage Four: Adjustment

As the initial impact of a pastor's departure subsides, a church begins to adjust. Individuals and, when available, other pastoral staff share responsibilities that need to be done. Visiting the sick and newcomers can be accomplished by the deacons and delegated to those who will assist in this service. A neighboring pastor can be called for funerals or weddings. Other adjustments can be made that will boost a church's confidence that God will enable them to make it through this transition time. Getting used to other voices in the pulpit may be the biggest adjustment of all, but that is essential for the time when a new pastor arrives to be God's spokesman.

## Stage Five: Assessment

Between pastors a church should assess where it is spiritually, organizationally and financially. A teams' initial task is to address this question: "What does the Lord want our church to become?" Out of serious reflection and interaction on this matter comes a specific guideline regarding the kind of leadership that needs to be sought in the new pastor.

A church should assess its weaknesses as well as its strengths; its facilities as well as its activities; its opportunities as well as its difficulties. Be careful, however, that you do not spend inordinate time on the negative. Look back long enough to evaluate honestly and confess seriously, then look ahead to the biblical expectations God has for the church. That will lead you into--

## Stage Six: Anticipation

In Acts 13, Paul reviews how Samuel located David who was God's choice for Israel's leadership. The Lord's confirmation of that choice was: "I have found David . . . a man after my own heart; he will do everything I want him to do" (verse 22). God will supply the man after His own heart to do His will in your church. It may involve extensive searching and intensive praying-- but God will meet the need of a serving and obedient people (Philippians 4:19)!

The anticipation stage can actually be a thrilling time in the life of the church. It is a time for new beginnings, another chance to do great things, and an opportunity to evaluate the church and its ministries. It may be just what the church needs to get beyond the status quo.

## Stage Seven: Approach

At this point the church is approaching its "destination," i.e. the calling of their next pastor. Candidates have been processed, interviewed, and observed. The Pastoral Discovery Team has narrowed down their choice to one or two men. It seems that God is about ready to introduce His choice to His congregation.

It is very important not to "drop the ball" at this point. Church unity and clarity of purpose is paramount at this juncture. While there is light at the end of the tunnel, you are still in the tunnel. Wait on God, and enjoy the descent to the runway- you are almost there!

## Stage Eight: Acquisition

The day will come when a pastor senses the call of the Great Shepherd, the eager invitation of a congregation and the tug of his own heart and will join the shepherding team of your flock! Be united and excited for that new chapter in the life of your church.

When you acquire your new pastor, love him, pray for him, respect him, generously support him, and cooperate with him. God's Word is clear:

> *"Now we ask you, brothers, to respect those who work hard among you, who are over you in the Lord and who admonish you. Hold them in the highest regard in love because of their work. Live in peace with each other" (1 Thessalonians 5:12,13).*

> *"Obey your leaders and submit to their authority. They keep watch over you as men who must give an account. Obey them so that their work will be a joy, not a burden, for that would be of no advantage to you" (Hebrews 13:17).*

And don't forget to thank God for how He led and sustained you through the phases of transition.

**Conclusion**

The following pages offer a step-by-step plan for arriving at that joyful day of a new beginning. Of course, a church has to adopt and develop procedures it prefers, but consider these suggested guidelines. At the outset the church will need to select a team to direct the process of finding the God's man for pastoral leadership.

**PASTORAL DISCOVERY TEAM- CHAPTER THREE *WORK IT OUT!***

Together determine the stages that you will work through (i.e. all of them, some of them, etc.). Now, describe in a paragraph or two how you will actually work through these eight stages:

_____

_____

_____

_____

_____

Based on your circumstances, what are some things that should be done before beginning the "next stage"?

_____

_____

_____

_____

Make a list of concerns, thoughts, or insights regarding each of the eight stages that will help you in this process, as well as help any candidates considering your church. Add other stages if necessary.

1. _____

2. _____

3. _____

4. _____

5. _____

6. _____

7. _____

8. _____

9. _____

10. _____

Together, as a team, take time to thank the Lord for your church, regardless of what stage you are in. Pray for your church, specifically regarding the eight stages of the Pastoral Discovery Process. Determine to walk through the process appropriately.

## Chapter Four
## Participation: The Exiting Pastor's Role
## in the Pastor Discovery Process

Many readers will find it strange that I say the exiting pastor has a role in the process of pastoral discovery. This is a new and radical idea. Or is it new? Didn't Moses have a role in calling Joshua? Didn't Paul prepare Timothy? Didn't Jesus groom Peter? There is both biblical and practical precedent for a leader to be involved in the calling of his successor.

While it is not appropriate for every congregation to engage in this stage of the process, those churches that are losing a greatly-loved and well-respected pastor may surely benefit from his active involvement as he "passes the torch."

### Progress is Always a Process

John Maxwell says, "Success is a journey, not a destination." In other words, *progress* (success) is always in *process* (journey). No church ever "arrives." A healthy church, which has almost always (if not always) been led by a great pastor, must see that when there is a pastoral vacancy (whether actual or anticipated), a leader should be involved in seeking his successor. This is a touchy subject, to say the least, but it is a doable and effective way to discover a new pastor.

### Success Has a Successor

This is a principle that almost all churches overlook. A person or organization has not truly been successful if the organization fails to secure a leader, after the departure of an effective leader, who can take them to the next level of the journey.

How is it a success when a church grows under the leadership of a dynamic pastor, only to decline immediately after his departure? Has a church succeeded when it reverts back to unhealthy habits after their effective pastor leaves? Was the church going the right direction if they go way off track when a new captain takes the wheel? These seemingly rhetorical questions yield the same not-so-rhetorical answer: such churches haven't truly been successful.

How can church leaders and a Pastoral Discovery Team ensure that a healthy church will *stay* healthy? How can successes prepare for successors? These questions must be answered in light of two entities: 1) the church seeking a pastor and; 2) the exiting pastor.

## Successor Steps for Churches

The church that desires to be healthy and stay healthy must take intentional steps to do so. Here are a few summary considerations:

- Don't build the church around a particular pastor or other person.

- Grow a church that is purpose-driven, not pastor-driven or personality-driven.

- Have a plan for pastoral succession in place long before the pastor departs.

- Include the current pastor in the succession plan. No one knows the church or its needs better than the pastor.

- Decide on a pastoral profile before entertaining résumés for your pastor's replacement.

- Don't discount the idea of your current pastor selecting, or at least strongly suggesting a successor.

- Don't automatically assume that your pastor's replacement should be a current staff member.

- Don't automatically assume that your pastor's replacement should *not* be a current staff member.

- Strongly discourage a retiring pastor from remaining in the congregation.

- If the date of a pastor's departure is roughly known, begin the succession process as soon as one year before the departure.

- Consider a transition-succession, where the current pastor remains for a predetermined time to mentor and orientate the succeeding pastor, after which the predecessor leaves.

- Allow the succeeding pastor to select his own pastoral staff, even if that means the resignations of current staff.

- Don't fail to involve your denominational or associational leaders in the process. They have generally acquired much collective wisdom over the years.

- Don't do anything regarding the process in a vacuum. Churches that are isolated or insulated from other churches usually make more mistakes calling a pastor.

- Don't view yourselves as *"hiring* a replacement," but rather see yourselves as *"calling* a successor".

- Get everything in writing.

- Pray and fast; pray and fast some more; pray and... Well, you get the picture.

As with all points made in this book, these steps must be applied in context; i.e. each church must determine how to flesh out these principles in their own context. If all these steps are not for you, don't throw the baby out with the bath water- use what you can.

**Successor Steps for Pastors**

The pastor who is appropriately exiting a church must also be intentional when it comes to preparing the church for his replacement. Here are some tips:

- Relinquish any insecurities or ego problems. There is no room for that in this process.

- Teach your church leaders the 17 *Successor Steps of Churches* (see above).

- Work with the leaders of the church to develop a transition plan.

- Prepare yourself for your departure.

- Know when to leave; don't stay too long.

- Know when to stay; don't leave too soon.

- Lead strategically, knowing that your time is limited.

- Make decisions and create outcomes that you could live with yourself for the long term.

- Prepare your family for the transition process.

- Get your financial house in order so you won't be limited in your options for your own transition, or be tempted to stay because of financial constraints.

- Prepare your staff for a potential successor.

- Be willing to do hard and uncomfortable things to prepare your church for transition.

- Always have what is best for your church, not your "career," in mind.

- Get everything regarding transition and departure in writing. It's not so much that people are dishonest, but that they forget or don't understand.

- Be prepared to be highly involved in the transition process (see the previous 17 steps).

- Pray and fast; pray and fast; pray and...

Again, while I am aware that many churches will be tempted to "skip" this chapter, it will be beneficial to at least prayerfully consider the principles set forth here. If a church can successfully utilize the wisdom, input, and participation of a departing pastor, it will generally result in less anxiety for the church, and a more effective choice of a new pastor. The key, again, is application to context.

**PASTORAL DISCOVERY TEAM- CHAPTER FOUR *WORK IT OUT!***

Together determine how the exiting pastor will or will not be involved in the process of pastoral discovery.

_____
_____
_____
_____
_____

Based on your circumstances, what are some things that should be done before beginning this process?

_____
_____
_____
_____
_____

Make a list of concerns, thoughts, or insights regarding this vital step that will help you in this process, as well as help any candidates considering your church. Add other stages if necessary.

1. _____

2. _____

3. _____

4. _____

5. _____

6. _____

7. _____

8. _____

9. _____

10. _____

Together, as a team, take time to thank the Lord for your church, regardless of your relationship with the exiting pastor. Pray for your church, specifically regarding the involvement (or lack thereof) of your exiting pastor. Determine to walk through the process appropriately.

# CHAPTER FIVE
## Organization: How to Organize Your Pastoral Search Team

"A committee," goes the humorous old definition, "is a group of the unfit, chosen by the unwilling to do the unnecessary." Another old adage is, "A camel is a horse made by a committee." The committee in your church that is commissioned with the responsibility of locating a pastoral candidate, however, should be the "fit," chosen by the "supportive" to do what is very "necessary." This team, for the purposes of this manual, shall not be called a "pastoral search committee" or "pulpit committee," but rather the "Pastoral Discovery Team." The word "team" is more descriptive of what this body really is. "Discovery" is better than "search," because God already knows who your next pastor is; it's simply up to you to discover who he is! In creating your Pastoral Discovery Team (PDT) you will need to . . .

### 1. Determine a Purpose for the PDT

The purpose of the PDT is to discern God's will for a pastoral candidate to present to your church family. This man is God's servant to help you grow to maturity in Christ and equip you for effective ministry. Pastor-teachers are gifted "to prepare God's people for works of service, so that the body of Christ may be built up until we all reach unity in the faith and in the knowledge of the Son of God and become mature, attaining to the whole measure of the fullness of Christ" (Ephesians 4:11-12). This means that the primary task of the PDT is to discern God's will through the principles of His Word, the persistent prayer of God's people, the perspective of godly leadership, providential circumstances, and the persuasion of God's Spirit and the peace of God.

### 2. Determine the Size of the PDT

The number of people on the PDT should not necessarily be a matter of church size. A team can be too large to meet easily and to function smoothly. It can also be too small to be adequately representative. A PDT of five to seven seems ideal (five being the author's preference). Some suggest that an odd number is important in case of tie votes. It is to be hoped that the team will enjoy a sweet spirit of pulling together to discover God's man and not need to break ties by a single vote. If the group is much larger, bear in mind the factors of reproducing résumés, listening to recordings and contacting members for special meetings.

## 3. Determine the Representation of PDT

Who should be represented on the PDT? Your constitution may decree the makeup of the team. It may even specify that the deacons or elders become the team. If it doesn't, it is wise for the boards to be represented as well as the membership at large.

Since a pastor's ministry must also be responsive to the spiritual needs of women, it may be appropriate that the female perspective be represented. If the deacons or elders function as the PDT, some ladies -- perhaps deacons' wives or elders' wives -- could meet as advisors when a couple is being interviewed. The prospect's wife would probably be more at ease having other women present.

Some qualifications for the members of the Pastoral Discovery Team are:

- A team member should be, above all, a person of spiritual maturity. The task of choosing a pastor under the congregational system demands a high level of spiritual maturity.

- A team member must have the respect of the congregation. This may be already apparent because of the offices he or she already holds. The need for credibility is self-evident in a system that allows a few to speak for the whole.

- Anyone who accepts the appointment should be committed to give the time and devotion required in the performance of the task. Make no mistake about it; a great amount of time is required to do the job well.

- The potential team person should know the church well.

- As a <u>group</u>, the team members should be compatible so they will work and travel well together.

## 4. Determine the Task of the PDT

A chairperson who is spiritually and emotionally mature should be elected by the PDT, unless chosen by the congregation at the time of appointments. The significant nature of this task points to choosing a godly person who is respected as a spiritual leader within the congregation. A secretary to keep accurate minutes of each meeting is necessary. This person also may handle correspondence, or the chairperson may prefer doing it. The contact person who is to be receiving résumés and giving updates should also be decided. Prompt and courteous correspondence is crucial for representing Christ and your local church to prospective pastoral candidates.

Travel is often involved to hear prospective candidates. Certain members of the PDT should be available for this purpose, if the whole team does not do it. It is usually beneficial for mates to join their spouses on trips to hear men, if the committee does not go as a unit. Going as couples, where possible, gives a more normal appearance in the church visited, and it allows for a dual reaction to be brought back for evaluation.

## 5. Determine the Meeting Schedule of the PDT

Each who serves must commit priority time to this priority task. Meetings of the PDT should be agreed upon for everyone's convenience. Meet regularly on a specified day even if no major decisions will be made. Prayer and discussion about your goals is important for fusing together divergent personalities and infusing each with the sense of God's will. Of course there may be occasions for special meetings as well. Agree on a concluding time for each session. A late-night marathon tends sometimes to elicit more sharp tempers than sharp thinking.

Here are some more thoughts for clarifying the roles of the Pastoral Discovery Team:

*Dr. Leonard Hill, [past] managing editor to the Baptist Program, stresses the need to clarify what the committee is to do. Few churches have job descriptions for their pulpit committees. "As a result," says Hill in his booklet Your Work on the Pulpit Committee, "most pulpit committees are forced to wander rather aimlessly in a never-never land— bombasted on one side for exceeding their authority; sternly criticized on the other for not assuming enough responsibility."*

To avoid hard feelings and to give stability and assurance to the task, the team may well suggest clarification of its role and have it confirmed by the church.

Understanding in six areas ought to be reached:

- Is the team responsible for obtaining pulpit supply and/or an interim pastor?

- How much is the team expected to do toward securing a pastor? For instance, is it simply to locate men to preach before the church or is it to do whatever is necessary until it is ready to recommend one choice as pastor?

- Concerning such things as salary, housing, moving expense, and so forth—how much is to be determined by church action and how much is to be left to the discretion of the team? Are these to be decided before the discovery process begins or is the team expected to make recommendations about such matters to the church at whatever time seems best?

- Has the church outlined some basic qualifications a prospective pastor must have or is this to be left entirely to the wisdom of the team?

- How much money will the church provide for Pastoral Discovery Team? What kind of accounting for expense funds is expected of the team?

- Is there a limit on the amount of time the team will have to do its work?

## 6. Determine the Budget for the PDT

Postage, phone calls, travel expenses -- perhaps copy machine fees -- should be projected costs for carrying out responsibilities. Members of this group should not be expected to absorb these costs themselves. Encourage a fund to be established for moving expenses, which could be substantial. You should also plan on reimbursing the candidate. That reimbursement might involve air flight and motel. The reason for doing this at the outset is so that all the normal salary and pastoral costs are not consumed in other church projects. Also, when there is a healthy, growing fund, a team can reach out further in its quest for a quality pastor.

## 7. Determine the Procedures of the PDT

Is the PDT responsible for obtaining pulpit supply or securing an interim pastor? This must be determined by the church at the time the PDT is formed. It is usually desirable for this to be the team's task, so preaching engagements can be easily coordinated.

The value of an interim pastor is that he is able to provide a more balanced spiritual diet for God's flock. The right man can sense special needs and develop his pulpit ministry to be of maximum help. It also avoids the constant change of personnel in the pulpit. Generally, the man you ask to be the interim is not to be a potential candidate. If a number of people want him to be permanent, this could work at cross purposes with the efforts of the team. Essentially, the role of the interim is to prepare the congregation for its new pastor. A retired pastor may be an ideal interim pastor.

There is increasing emphasis today on the role and value of an intentional interim ministry. The PDT may want to research this concept early on in the discovery process. See Appendix Nine.

Here are some more thoughts about procedures (adapted from Emmett Johnson):

- Begin work as soon as the team is established. Since the work will often take four to six months it is important to begin soon. There is sometimes apprehension about beginning a search for a new pastor while the pastor is still in the church, especially if he is well-liked. A pastor who cares about the ministry of the church will not object if the church moves ahead to find his successor. Under normal circumstances it is unnecessary to delay the work of the PDT until the pastor has left the church.

- Before any work begins the team must become a single working unit through a period of sharing, scripture reading and prayer together. Get used to each other. Covenant to work together. You are going to be together a great deal. Mr. Ken McQuere, Directory of Moody Bible institute Alumni Associates, observed: "The constitution cannot give to the team one needed ingredient—unity. The members should come together as a team without any superstars wanting to make all the decisions."

- Agree together to keep reports and files on pastors and churches confidential. Many pastors have had their reputations tarnished by the airing of confidential reports about them—true or not.

- Further, sometimes merely because a man's name is mentioned as being under consideration, the news has filtered back to his own church and his people jump to the conclusion that he wants to leave and he is caught in the bind of all that may seem to mean. Keep the names of the candidates you are considering confidential.

- Review your constitution and by-laws as to any specific procedures which are demanded, e.g., the length of prior notice to the congregation as to the coming of a candidate and the calling of the pastor, the percentage of vote he must have for a call, etc. This will avoid embarrassment and parliamentary conflict later on.

- Review and agree upon (a) the steps to be taken, (b) the information of the church and its ministry that the team will prepare, and (c) what will be expected from each candidate.

- Plan periodic reports to the congregation. Because one of the problems in the interim between pastors is the seeming silence of the Pastoral Discovery Team, it is important that the chairperson periodically assures the church of the team's hard work and at the same time, asks for prayer support (See *Appendix 6* for an excellent prayer pledge card to be used in a morning worship service). Announcements in the bulletin and church paper of Pastoral Discovery Team meetings assure the church that the team has not given up. A letter to the congregation at the onset of the team's work, enunciating the procedures would be helpful.

- If not set forth in the constitution or in the church's instructions to the team, the decision to present one name only should be agreed upon. This does not mean that in the early stages of their work several prospects will not be examined.

The practice of considering one man at a time commends itself in two ways:

- First, candidates are not measured against each other, but against a common standard. This standard should be developed by your team after studying the Scriptures and the needs of your church.

- Second, it aids harmony and unity within the church. One preacher is not pitted against another, with some factions in the church desiring one man, the rest another. The situation is even more likely to promote disunity when more than one man is asked to preach in view of a call before the church makes a decision.

If a church and team does decide to have more than one man candidate before the vote to call is taken, each candidate should be informed of the procedure. Very few men will enter the lists!

- Try to make the Pastoral Discovery Team's recommendation of a candidate unanimous. Joseph I. Chapman writes, "We also urge the team not to recommend a person to the church until, in clear conscience, the entire team can join in the recommendation. It is our conviction that for a man to come to the church with one or more members of the team in opposition to his coming is to lay the foundation for dissension and strife that can seldom be overcome."

There is the gap between pastorates that must also concern the Pastoral Discovery Team. While it surely is the task of the elder or deacon board (or the church board) to provide for counsel to church members who need it and to see that calls are made and the pulpit filled, the team should be sure that this ground rules hold; namely that persons who speak during the interim—whether as pulpit supply, interim speaker or interim pastor—not be considered for the pastorate.

## 8. Determine the Accountability of the PDT

The PDT should regularly inform and consult with the spiritual leadership of the church (that is, the elders or deacons). Their spiritual insight and oversight should be an integral part of the search process.

The congregation should receive regular updates concerning the pastoral discovery process. Their prayer and participation are important. The more they are involved in the process, the more likely they will be supportive of the conclusion.

Questions for the PDT to decide also need to include: What steps will be followed with each name presented? How will interviews with prospective candidates be conducted? (See sample questions in Appendix 1.)

## CONCLUSION

The success of the Pastoral Discovery Team in many ways will determine the future success of the church! By all means elect or appoint only the best persons for the task, and do everything to insure that the team is lead and functions properly. "Excellence" is the key. God deserves that, and so does your church.

## PASTORAL DISCOVERY TEAM- CHAPTER FIVE *WORK IT OUT!*

List the members of the PDT. Beside each name write a brief description of that person (their role in the church, their "expertise," etc., as well as contact information, i.e. email, phone, etc.).

1. _____
2. _____
3. _____
4. _____
5. _____
6. _____
7. _____

List the "officers" of the PDT:

1. Chair Person: _____
2. Vice Chair: _____
3. Secretary:_____
4. Other: _____

Briefly describe how you will execute the eight responsibilities listed above:

1. _____

2. _____

3. _____

4. _____

5. _____

6. _____

7. _____

8. _____

Together, as a team, take time to thank the Lord for your PDT, individually praying for each member. Pray for your church, specifically regarding the involvement of your PDT members and other leaders who will participate in this process.

# CHAPTER SIX
## Articulation: Determining the Basics

Your first need is not to gather a pile of résumés but to begin a process of self-study in which you research church preferences, assess needs and secure basic information.

### 1. Conduct a Poll

Some teams prepare a detailed list of the various phases of pastoral ministry (preaching, discipleship, leadership development, counseling, visiting, etc.) and request opinions. Other teams utilize church consulting firms to pursue a comprehensive analysis of the church. Many find it productive to ask only two questions on a bulletin insert, church website, or social network page, and request responses:

- What qualities do you hope and pray for in the next pastor?

- What major emphases do you sense our church needs to pursue in future ministry?

Avoid making your opinion poll too wordy or too analytical.

Scheduling about five minutes within the morning service for worshippers to write their responses dramatically emphasizes the seriousness of pastoral selection. Further, it provides a period of corporate prayer with the largest gathering of the flock. After the prayer and the paperwork, collect the sheets. If you allow people to do this at home, you probably cannot expect more than a 30% response. Some extra sheets can be provided on a table for those who may have been absent. Let none feel excluded from contributing input. Increase the response by using your church's website and Facebook page.

Additionally, it is beneficial to urge people to express their thoughts to any of the members of the team during the entire search process. Repeat this periodically in print, emails, text messages, social networks, and through pulpit announcements. Involving the church family in the search process encourages their prayers and their ownership of the outcome.

## 2. Organize Information into Operating Guidelines

When you have the pulse of the people, you can assemble the information needed to complete a "Church Information Form." This is a simple tool that enables appropriate referrals to be offered. This allows for an initial exchange of information and for the man to be praying along with the team for God's direction.

## 3. Develop a Pastoral Profile

As procedures and standards are adopted they should be listed for use in screening résumés. For example, there may be matters of doctrinal sensitivity that need to be taken into consideration. Or perhaps a style of pastoral leadership is the felt need of the majority. Certain skills or emphases may be preferred. Age and experience may be deemed important in the selection process. Significant factors should become checkpoints for appraising each résumé. This will influence choices on the basis of predetermined expectations rather than momentary emotions.

## 4. Clarify Your Ministry

The team should also secure or develop a working description of the purpose for which the church exists. Sometimes this is termed "mission clarification." Either your team or the deacons/elders should compile a realistic, exciting expression of your church's task. You might cover the areas of worship, education, outreach, etc. Each working group within the church should be asked to convey in one or two paragraphs what it sees as the purpose of the church and its role in helping to fulfill that purpose. Specific objectives should be gathered from each source and condensed into a brief clarification of the church's mission in the world and in the community. Reduce that to a few pages, duplicate and have available as part of the packet for prospective candidates.

Yes, this project will take some valuable time but will be immensely helpful in evaluating each man you consider. You cannot know if a man is right for your church if you do not have a clear focus of what your ministry really is. A prospective candidate has a right to inquire about what the church sees as its function. He should not be expected to bring the goals and guidelines; he ought to be secured because he is challenged with what the church perceives her mission to be. A good pastor will be attracted and motivated by a well-conceived set of objectives that show vision and direction.

## 5. Develop a Ministry Expectation

This is sometimes called a job description in the business world. It is essential that you think through and list specific responsibilities and policies regarding pastoral function. This will help to avoid later confusion and clashes. Built into this document ought to be a plan for performance review or ministry evaluation. A man should know, for instance, that annually the elders/deacons or a pastoral relations team will share reactions to his ministry and allow for any mid-course adjustments that may be wise. Having this kind of prior agreement with a pastor can head off many of the ugly, damaging conflicts that so often scar a church.

Whatever final list of expectations you arrive at should be adopted by the church so it has agreement and authority.

## 6. Prepare an Adequate Financial Package

Note: Chapter Twelve deals entirely with remuneration. Read that in conjunction with the suggestions offered here.

You will need to have in hand a clear grasp of what your church is prepared to invest in pastoral care. This should include a meeting with the board responsible for this part of your budget. Working out a suitable financial package to offer the candidate may require overcoming the traditions of the past, the uncertainty of the future and the confusion that sometimes surrounds the pastor's "pay package". A pastor with the training and experience your church needs is worthy of generous support -- even if it stretches your faith. Most churches are offering their pastors the opportunity to purchase their own homes. Consideration should be given to the need for building financial equity for the pastor and his family.

Consider the biblical responsibilities for supporting elders who devote time to preaching and teaching: "The elders who direct the affairs of the church well are worthy of double honor, especially those whose work is preaching and teaching . . . 'The worker deserves his wages'" (1 Timothy 5:17).

Trust in God's provision for your future and growth potential! God will honor a commitment to be generous toward His servants in full-time ministry!

In studying the whole financial picture, it may be helpful to divide every expense regarding a pastor into two categories.

1. *Professional Costs*.

Auto expenses, cellphone, ministry expenses, book and journal costs, internet usage and other technologies, continuing education tuition, national and state conference fees--these kinds of items are not salary. These are expenses that should be recognized as essential to maintaining pastoral service. They should not have to be paid out of a pastor's salary. A car, for example, is as essential for ministry as a telephone.

Check current tax laws to make sure that the alignment of expenses in this category are labeled and expended to the pastor's tax advantage. Your denomination or associational center probably has resources to assist you in this area, por consult a tax professional that is familiar with church law.

## 2. *Personal Compensation.*

A base salary, fair rental value of the parsonage (or housing allowance, if he prefers to own his residence), utilities, Social Security allowance (because a pastor, considered self-employed, has to pay more than the average employee), and a tax-sheltered retirement plan. These are items involved in income. With changing tax laws, these items too should be checked out for best procedure.

As you review these matters, keep in mind the biblical principles of pastoral support, such as I Timothy 5:17,18 and I Corinthians 9:7-14. Most servants of God are reluctant to emphasize their personal needs, but their effectiveness in providing for their family releases them to focus on the ministry.

To arrive at an adequate salary you should know what the median income in your community is. Check with your local government for this information. Some churches also average the incomes of the leadership in the congregation. And, of course, you need to take into account what a pastor's needs are based on his family situation and insurance and retirement considerations.

There's one more item that may need review . . .

## 7. **Look at Your Vacation Offer**

Are you offering an adequate amount of time for vacation? Actually, this is one of the least expensive and most appreciated benefits you can make available to a man considering your church. The unique demands of the pastorate can exact an enormous toll on the man of God. The stress and burnout casualties in ministry are mounting. A generous vacation, even if longer than the average member may get, seems wise when the following values are considered.

- Emotional value--to help a man cope with the drain of confronting all sorts of human crises in the lives of those he seeks to help.

- Physical value--to give time to renew the strength that has been spent in the hard work and long hours.

- Spiritual value--to recharge a man's spiritual energy and allow him to be ministered to for a few weeks.

- Family value--to reward a family for those many evenings without Dad when they shared him with others through the year.

- Church value--to enable a pastor to bring back fresh perspectives gained from reading, praying and reflecting.

Four weeks of vacation is what most churches provide. And be sure to allow him to divide his time away into two packages, if that fits his finances and needs best. If he chooses to spend some of that time home, do not bother him with church business. In fact, if you want a man's vacation time to be of maximum value to the family and to the church, make it possible for him to vacate--to get away. Perhaps a recreational vehicle or cottage on the lake can be loaned.

## CONCLUSION:

These issues are important. In many cases, expert opinion, outside help, and plain old-fashioned advice is in order! Make sure that this step in the process is taken seriously, especially the issues dealing with taking care of your pastor. It is the right thing to do, and God will honor it.

**PASTORAL DISCOVERY TEAM- CHAPTER SIX *WORK IT OUT!***

Assign research and follow-up on the seven headings above and:

1. _____

2. _____

3. _____

4. _____

5. _____

6. _____

7. _____

Briefly describe how you will execute the seven steps listed above:

1. _____

2. _____

3. _____

4. _____

5. _____

6. _____

7. _____

What other needs and issues need to be considered at this point?

_____

_____

Together, as a team, take time to thank the Lord for resources He has given your church. Pray for your church, specifically regarding taking care of your next pastor. Pray for the leaders and lay-persons who will participate in this process.

## CHAPTER SEVEN
## Communication: How to Secure Prospects

When a pastoral vacancy occurs names are often volunteered from various individuals. You will need to secure other names by diligent search. That's why it is a good idea to think of your selves as a "Pastoral Discovery Team." Of course, this entails both toil and time. If you were Methodists, for instance, the replacement would be simple. A bishop would assign your new pastor. Baptists, however, prefer self-government. The choice of a pastor must be yours. Make your autonomy work--even if it takes longer than you might desire. Your denominational or associational staff do not seek to impose any pressures or preferences upon you, only to serve and assist in referring competent possibilities for your consideration.

### 1. Plan on Names from Friends

Receive names that individuals may offer. Do not ask for them, but do not be indifferent to them. While this may not be the best method for name procurement, the sovereignty of God can certainly cause the name of His choice to be referred from any source. When names are offered, request as much information as possible. Ask each person that suggests a name why they feel this person would make a good pastor of your church. If the name submitted is a family member or relative, realize that honest objectivity may be affected by that fact.

Leonard Hill's insight is invaluable as he shares the specific characteristics of a good recommendation.

- A good pastoral candidate recommendation will be made by a person whose integrity and judgment the church can trust; one who is well enough acquainted with the man he is recommending and the pastor-less church in order to make a judgment.

- The recommendation will reveal how much the person making the recommendation knows about the prospective pastor; how close a contact he has with him and his past and present work.

- It will indicate how much the person making the recommendation knows about the church seeking a pastor ---its needs and opportunities.

- It will reveal the prospective pastor's strong points and weaknesses; giving specific as well as general information.

- It will explain why, in light of the recommender's knowledge of the prospective pastor and pastor-less church, he thinks the man is suited to the church.

- The recommendation will not attempt to place the Holy Spirit's stamp of approval on the man recommended, unless the recommender has a definite, deep-seated conviction he should do so.

## 2. Expect Some to Offer Their Own Names

If pastors or those who desire pastorates volunteer their own names, be considerate but cautious. If a man graciously asks to be considered and does not have any referral service to make the contact, give him fair consideration and very thorough evaluation. Or you might refer him to an associational office and suggest that his name be channeled through that office. This allows an unbiased associational executive to help in ascertaining his appropriateness for referral to your church.

## 3. Contact Schools (Colleges and Seminaries)

Christian colleges and seminaries have referral departments. Contacting these schools can make available recent or pending graduates that might be suitable or older, experienced alumni. One must assess the graduates on their individual merits and convictions and not exclusively upon the reputation of the school from which they were graduated. The church should stick to school s that have doctrinal statements that are in alignment with their own.

## 4. Look to Your Association

Denominations and associations are prepared to serve you in referring capable men. Each regional ministry center maintains a file of potential candidates who have completed standard forms, supplied the same key information and signed the doctrinal statement of the association and ministerial ethics statements. Your associational executive may be able to offer personal insight about these men. He also knows some who may not be looking for relocation but whose fine ministries and length of service commend them for consideration.

The advantage of working through your regional ministry center is that their staff gets to know your church and your needs by personal contacts with you. The better they understand your desires, the better they can help you in your pastoral search. So keep them well-informed, and don't hesitate to call them whenever there is need for his assistance.

## 5. Look to Your Current Pastoral Staff

While a church must be cautious when considering a current staff member for the senior pastor's position, it may be appropriate to look into the possibility. Often inner-church politics, inner-staff conflict or competition, or a lack of objectivity concerning a "home-grown" candidate can create trouble for the church. In most cases it is not appropriate to consider a current staff member, but if the Lord seems to be leading the church in that direction, enter the process carefully and with guidance from the regional director or some other trusted mentor of the church. Be careful if any of the following conditions apply:

- A staff member is "pursuing" the position

- An elder, deacon, or other church member is "pushing for" the staff member

- Hiring the staff member is the "road of least resistance"

- The staff member is not adequately trained or has inadequate experience

- The staff member has family members in the church

- The exiting pastor does not recommend the staff member as his successor

- The church is not in general "agreement" about the possible calling of the staff person

- The regional director or other associational or denominational leader does not recommend the staff member

- The calling of a current staff member violates your church's polity, constitution, or other protocols

- Etc.

There are many examples of successful "promotions" of associate pastors to the senior pastor position, but there are probably more examples of unsuccessful ones. If your church is determined to move in this direction, do so with caution and in with much humility. If you are not willing to seek and heed the advice of a trusted "outside" mentor or consultant, you may be heading in the wrong direction.

## 6. Pastoral Placement and Referral Ministries

There are many organizations that specialize in pastoral placement services. Most of these, of course, require a fee of some sort, but often the investment is well worth it! The best place to find such organizations is through your regional or national office, or by surfing the internet. The advantage to such a service is that it will open up a whole wide world of potential candidates. The disadvantage is that it will yield a lot of applicants who are outside the church's doctrinal and associational perimeters. Like any avenue of referrals, enter such an endeavor with caution.

## 7. Other Sources for Pastoral Candidates

Write down any other sources you may know for pastoral candidates:

_____

_____

_____

_____

_____

_____

## CONCLUSION

As stated before, God already has someone to pastor your church; it is up to you to "discover" him. Trust the Lord, bathe the matter in constant prayer and fasting, and sincerely expect great things in the process. God is going to do great things in your church!

**PASTORAL DISCOVERY TEAM- CHAPTER SEVEN *WORK IT OUT!***

Describe your team's response to the seven sources of pastoral candidates:

1. _____

2. _____

3. _____

4. _____

5. _____

6. _____

7. _____

Briefly describe how you will utilize (or not utilize) the seven sources listed above:

1. _____

2. _____

3. _____

4. _____

5. _____

6. _____

7. _____

What others needs and issues need to be considered at this point? _____

_____

Together, as a team, take time to thank the Lord for sources of pastoral candidates He has revealed to you. Pray for your church, specifically regarding the sources of referrals for your next pastor. Pray for the members of the Pastoral Discovery Team.

# CHAPTER EIGHT
## Evaluation: How to Handle Résumés

Well prepared résumés will give you enough information to acquaint you with a man's training, family and philosophy of ministry. When you are comparing a number of résumés at a time, it may be confusing as to which man is best for your church. If you have listed your expectations and qualifying factors as suggested earlier, then each résumé can be evaluated in the light of these. Be careful, though, that you are not so idealistic that you are not realistic.

Perhaps a pastor's preaching is not as forceful as you would like, but his pastoral skills are strong. You may prefer a younger man, but a certain brother meets all other standards. Maybe a good man has a physical factor that overshadows an otherwise promising capability. Somebody once pointed out that a man in trouble with the law, run out of town, suffering a serious physical malady, unmarried and over fifty would not check out very well with most committees today. Therefore, a man by the name of Paul, were he alive today, would be bypassed!

*Here are some orderly steps for processing résumés*

### 1. Adopt a Standard Form

If you receive a promising résumé that is not based on a standard form or in a standard format, you may want to send him a blank copy of it and explain that this is the body of information needed to make a fair assessment. This enables you to have the same data on each person being considered. It also has the additional value of determining the man's doctrinal and functional alignment with your church's chosen association.

Experience has revealed that it is wise to discuss names under serious consideration with your regional association executive, if he has not referred them. Sometimes he is aware of something you might need to know.

## 2. Be Courteous

Each résumé represents a man's life and ministry. Give it both consideration and courtesy. Write a brief letter or email (if that is appropriate) to those you do not wish to consider further at this time. Sometimes a Pastoral Discovery Team is led back to a person not initially preferred.

## 3. Ascertain Availability

Send a letter or email of inquiry to those you wish to consider further and ascertain whether they are interested in being considered. (Note sample letter in Appendix 2.) If you are extremely interested in a particular candidate, you may want to simply call him. Circumstances change in the course of time, and the person may not choose to move or may have already determined a move. Make your letter, email or call personal. (A form letter does not convey a high level of interest). You might include a bulletin or brochure, but explain that other information will be sent if the candidate becomes a viable, suitable consideration. Ask for a reply within a week or two. Don't let men who fail to answer their mail, email, or voicemail promptly delay the arduous task of the pastoral discovery process.

## 4. Keep Looking

Do not feel discouraged if none of the original group of résumés seems to pinpoint the man you seek. Request other résumés. Additional names come in regularly, and perhaps the right one for you will be in the next batch of possibilities sent to you. Often many names and many months are required to locate the pastor gifted and called to serve the Lord among you. It has been my experience that most churches, including small ones, will receive scores of résumés. I know of at least three churches running under 100 in attendance that received over 150 résumés. If you are only receiving a handful of résumés, something has gone wrong in the process. Discuss this as a team and adjust accordingly.

Be sure, however, that you give more than casual consideration to the selected résumés sent to you from your denomination or association. These are capable men, whom if you knew personally--even through a phone conversation-- might create appeal.

## 5. Respect confidences

Another caution needs to be stressed. Be very careful that you do not divulge confidential names and information outside the committee. A man's present position could be jeopardized if word got to his people prematurely that he was being considered elsewhere. This might create needless unrest in the church he serves. Also, if any negative evaluations are made or references secured, keep them tightly classified so as not to hurt a man and his ministry. Do not leave résumés, references or minutes lying around the church or a home where they can be read by non-team personnel. These should be carefully disposed of when no longer needed.

Additionally, in today's electronic age, be very careful not send emails to the wrong person, or to accidentally text-message the wrong candidate. Also, don't leave confidential information in voicemails. Not only are these mistakes embarrassing, but they can create severe problems.

## 6. Narrowing the List Down

Attempt to narrow the list of candidates down to six or less. Prayerfully review each person and his background, weighing the recommendations. A valuable exercise is to let each team member rank the top three against the standard you have set. When completed, let members tell why they have ranked them is this order. Often, the same candidates will consistently be listed as the top three. These names--- a maximum of six ---then become your list of candidates.

## CONCLUSION

The résumé is the "key" to successfully finding a pastor. It is the "first impression," the list of "credentials," the "snapshot" of the man, and the summary of his ministry and career. Treat résumés respectfully and honorably. As God continues to point you to His man, your future pastor's résumé will "rise to the top."

## PASTORAL DISCOVERY TEAM- CHAPTER EIGHT *WORK IT OUT!*

Describe your team's response to the top seven résumés you have received so far:

1. _____

2. _____

3. _____

4. _____

5. _____

6. _____

7. _____

List the ways you will apply the principles of chapter eight to your discovery process:

_____

_____

_____

_____

_____

_____

_____

What others needs and issues need to be considered at this point? _____

_____

Together, as a team, take time to thank the Lord for the résumés you have received so far. Pray for each man who has applied for the position. Pray for the team members of the Pastoral Discovery Team that they will have unity regarding discerning the potential candidates.

## CHAPTER NINE
## Preservation: How to Deal with Difficulties

"Not weary in well-doing" (Galatians 6:9) should earmark your discovery of a pastor. The devil may discourage you in many ways, and you may be tempted more than once to "throw in the towel." Sometimes months may go by with evidence of little or no progress. Some church members may grow discouraged, become critical of the Pastoral Discovery Team and even leave. This may not only threaten the survival of the team but also delay the arrival of a pastor.

What should you do if some of these symptoms arise? Immediately pursue four courses of action.

- Commit yourselves as a team to a renewed conviction that God promises to provide a shepherd for His flock (Jeremiah 23:4).

- Claim the gracious promise of Psalm 27:13-14: "I am still confident of this: I will see the goodness of the Lord in the land of the living. Wait for the Lord: be strong and take heart and wait for the Lord." And in Jeremiah 31:16 we read: "'Restrain your voice from weeping and your eyes from tears, for your work will be rewarded,' declares the Lord."

- Call the congregation to an intense week of prayer, honestly stating that limited progress has been achieved and that a significant spiritual breakthrough is needed. Meditating on a passage like Jeremiah 33 may set the tone for this period of prayer and heart-searching: "Call to me and I will answer you . . . I will bring health and healing . . . I will cleanse . . . They will be in awe and will tremble at the abundant prosperity and peace I provide . . ." (verses 3-9). In preparation for a new day of ministry, urge that everyone seek forgiveness where needed (I John 1:9) and fullness as needed (Ephesians 3:16-19). God may be waiting to get His people ready for the man as well as the man ready for the people.

- Contact your denomination or associational office and discuss the impasse that you may have. Perhaps a review of procedures and some redirection will enable you to go on to your goal. "Plans fail for lack of counsel" is the word of wisdom in Proverbs 15:22. Avail yourselves of the resources available to you.

- If you are an independent church with no associational connections, seek outside counsel from a veteran pastor, or church consultant. You should also contact churches of like faith that have recently gone through the pastoral discovery process and solicit ideas and assistance. They will be glad to help.

- Take special note of problems that seem systemic. Try to isolate the problem, and have a PDT meeting that focuses on nothing but the main problem. Allow for honest feedback, and be open up to any and all suggestions. Be creative.

- If you seem stuck in a rut, you may want to consider bringing some "fresh blood" into the PDT. Sometimes all it takes is one creative addition to the team to help you solve a problem and move forward.

Remember, God "founded" your church. It is His desire that your church not only survives, but also thrives! And your church cannot thrive without the right shepherd. So rest assured that God is going to get you through this tough time!

**PASTORAL DISCOVERY TEAM- CHAPTER NINE *WORK IT OUT!***

Describe your team's seven most discouraging and frustrating issues right now:

1. _____

2. _____

3. _____

4. _____

5. _____

6. _____

7. _____

List the ways you will apply the principles of chapter nine to the difficulties you are experiencing in the discovery process:

_____

_____

_____

_____

_____

_____

What others needs and issues need to be considered at this point? _____

_____

Together, as a team, take time to thank the Lord for the struggles you are going through, as this is an opportunity to prove your faith and see Him work miracles in your church! Pray for the team members of the Pastoral Discovery Team that they will have the peace of God through the tough times.

# CHAPTER TEN
## Determination: Selecting a Candidate

One of the most difficult things the Pastoral Discovery Team will have to do is select a candidate from the many résumés it will entertain. How does a team, from a pile of what may be dozens of résumés (one church I worked with of around 100 in attendance had 185), "narrow down" the choice to one or two potential candidates? Here is a little practical advice.

### 1. Use the Telephone

The telephone can be a valuable timesaver. Place a call to a man you desire to know better. This important phone visit can be pre-arranged for a time when all parties can participate. There are several "conference calling" services available, and a high-quality speaker phone works well, too. Conference calling services enable you to have team members participate from separate locations. The call should involve at least three team members and the prospect and his wife. Make this a friendly conversation in which you discuss your church, housing siruation, community and vision. Let them ask questions. Do not pursue heavy doctrinal matters at this point. Keep it casual and friendly. This phone visit will create a positive or negative impression of their personalities, attitudes and responses. This is much more effective than if one member of the committee does the phone interview, and it gives a broader basis of evaluation. The call need not be longer than 30 minutes to accomplish its purpose.

### 2. Email the Candidate

Email is a great tool to use when "interviewing" candidates. Often an email (following a "hard copy" letter) containing the general job description, profile of the church, etc., can be used as a way to determine interest on the part of the potential candidate. While this may have been taboo a few years ago, in today's electronic world, this is totally acceptable.

The key is to use email as an "interest discerning" method only. In other words, a formal interview, fact-finding interview, or attempt at meaningful communication must take place by phone or in person. Email may be used, however, to determine the "interest" of a candidate. This is a great time saver, and also serves as a "written record" of a candidate's interest (or lack thereof).

For example, if you have written a candidate expressing interest in him, and have not heard back from him, he may respond quickly to an email in which he can let you know whether or not he wants to pursue the position any further.

Email is not the *best* way to communicate; it is *a* way. Use it sparingly and use it appropriately. It may serve as a great tool at this point in the process.

### 3. Request a CD, DVD, or Audio or Video Download Link

Far wiser than prematurely visiting a man's church is to ask him for an audio or video recording that is typical of his preaching. If possible, obtain a CD or DVD that can be duplicated, or even better, get a link to a website with his recordings (like Sermon.net, YouTube, etc.). He may be able to email MP3, MP4, or other electronic files, but these can often be too large for email transmission. Listen for content, interest, delivery and style. Maybe even the length is important to you.

The best thing is to get a sample of the candidate's overall preaching style. For example, if the candidate is known to preach topically to a more general audience on Sunday morning, but more expositionally to a Christian audience on Sunday night, ask him for a sample of both. It is best to get three or four samples to better determine his skill and variety.

## 4. Interview Personally

If after the telephone visit and the recording evaluation, you are desirous of getting better acquainted with a prospect, invite him to meet with your team. In situations where this is not convenient, exchange information through email.

If you interview personally at this point or at a later time, certain essential questions need to be asked. List what you feel is important in determining the choice of a man. Appendix 1 suggests some items you may want to cover, using the "TEAM" approach.

Emmett Johnson offers this practical advice for helping your team to effectively interview prospects:

> *Questioning during interview should perhaps begin with a statement of his personal walk with God, general family background. Typical interview questions will also include what he (and his family) does for recreation, what he hopes to be doing a decade from now, the last six books he has read, continuing education program, his view of the church today, his frustrations about the ministry, what he likes to do best, what he is best at, his experiences in evangelism, his ideas about worship, his attitude toward missions, toward the denomination, his views on stewardship, his health, cooperation with other churches, participation in community programs and service organizations, his way of working with staff (volunteer and paid), his view of and participation in Christian education, his understanding of life style, does he assent to the statement of faith?*

Somewhere the discussion ought to arrive at an open view of what the church is like and what the church is looking for in its future and hence in the pastor they are calling.

- Is your church looking to the future? If it has a strong orientation to yesterday, this ought to come out. Few pastors are excited about turning the clock back to 1985.

- What are the current trends in the community or area? What changes in the community or area will demand a corresponding change in the church's mode of ministry?

- Is the church open to innovative forms of worship, like modern music and interpretive dance, or does it intend to remain traditional and more formal (which is okay)? Is your church willing to accept some changes?

- Who are the neighboring churches? What are they doing? What is the extent of cooperation with them?

The Pastoral Discovery Team ought also to come prepared to ask questions proposed by the candidate who, wanting to go behind the statistical facts, might ask such searching questions as:

- Why are you a member of _____ Baptist Church?

- What is the most important strength or asset of _____ Baptist?

- In terms of ministry and program, what do the members of _____ Baptist do?

- What new ministries or programs have been added recently or are under consideration?

- If you could change one thing at _____ Baptist, what would it be?

- If you could have one wish about the life, program, and ministry of this church come true, what would be your wish?

- If a twenty-nine year old teacher, his wife and their two children, ages five and three, moved to your community from Seattle next month and visited _____ Baptist Church on their own initiative, why might they decide to join? Why might they look elsewhere for a new church home?

- If one of your members died and left _____ Baptist $250,000 in her will with absolutely no restrictions on the use of the money, how do you think members would decide how the money should be used?

- What were the major goals that you as a congregation set for yourselves this year and how are you doing in reaching these?

- When was _____ Baptist at its peak in strength and vitality?

Rarely will the pastor ask all of them, but in the asking of only three he will get a good behind-the-scenes look at First Baptist. The committee should come prepared!

## 5. Prepare a Candidate Packet

Prior to a personal interview or for mailing or emailing purposes, assemble a packet of information. Include material that will give the candidate insight into your church and community. Also include a church constitution, statement of purpose, annual report (with salaries blacked out), church newsletter, pictures and description of church facilities. Information on schools will be of interest to those with school age children.

A letter at this point might also pose any specific doctrinal or practical questions that need clarification. Ask if the salary package is adequate and clear.

In corresponding with a potential candidate, it is usually wise to mail everything to his residence and mark it "confidential." If you are emailing electronic documents, verify that you have the appropriate email address. You do not want the package to go to the wrong person! The candidate may also prefer that you phone him at home or on his cell phone rather than at the church office.

Emmett Johnson offers these guidelines to help the team out when writing to a candidate (or candidates):

- *Write to the top six (or less) nominees to determine their willingness to have their names stand as candidates.*

- *Include the profile of the church (which ought also to include an attractive color photo of the church and facilities).*

- *Include a copy of The Constitution and By-Laws (if these are very old and about to be amended you may note what changes are in the making). If your statement of faith is greatly different than [that of your association], you may raise some problems for the prospective candidate. For instance, a church which states that members must subscribe to the pre-tribulation rapture position may be hard-pressed to find a pastor, not because there are not men who subscribe to this position, but because the pastor realizes that this would shut the membership door to many fine Christians.*

- *Usually it is wise not to include a copy of the Annual Report unless salaries and other costs for pastoral remuneration have been blacked out. These should be negotiable. The man you want, seeing a very low salary, may turn you own at this juncture, simply on that point, feeling that the Lord would not move him to a substantial cut in his present salary.*

- *Do not send a questionnaire. I always felt that when a questionnaire accompanied the initial inquiry I was being asked to apply for the job! This is not the case. You, as a team member representing the church, are asking him to consider being a candidate. There is a world of difference. Time will come later for candidates to fill out a questionnaire.*

- *Remember, the warmth of your letter, its neatness and style are all the reader has to judge your church by at this point. It is your first overture to him as a potential candidate. Make it do its work!*

- *Ask for a reply by a certain date, preferably within two weeks. If he writes and asks for more time, allow it. If you receive no answer within two weeks and if you feel he is an excellent choice, you may want to call him, asking him if any further information might help.*

## 6. Refer the Candidate to Your Church's Website

Your church's website or Facebook page may be the best sources of information for your candidate. There he can see an overview of your ministries, a profile of your community, biographies of your staff, pictures of your facilities, and a whole lot more. If your church does not have a website, the candidate may think you are "behind the times" and not relevant for your community. A sharp and well-done website says to a candidate, "We want to reach 21st Century people for Christ!"

## 7. Check References

This is a good time to check references. Please do not bother people with the task of giving a reference until you are impressively interested in a man. Write to or phone those whose names have been given in the résumé. If you pursue secondary references, be sure not to jeopardize the pastor's confidentiality. You do not want to jeopardize his present ministry.

Don't prepare too lengthy a reference form. (Note the sample reference letter in Appendix 3, which may also be used for phoning.) Those who give sensitive information often would rather give it verbally than in writing. It also allows for some discussion. If you mail a form, always enclose a stamped and addressed envelope for the reply. It is also appropriate to email the form.

7. **Visit and Observe**

The team should determine the most promising candidate from among the prospects considered and carefully checked. Give adequate time for discussion, prayer and unity. When one man seems to be the best choice, plan to visit his church to hear him preach, if possible. (If he is a student or minister not presently pastoring, perhaps he can be heard at a church willing to let him preach for that occasion.)

Visiting a man's place of ministry will offer an impression of the congregation, the impact of the service, the man's appearance and effectiveness in the pulpit. It is best that not more than two PDT members sit together. Otherwise it may be obvious that a "pastoral search committee" is visiting the church. If someone asks where you are from, give your home community and state that you are in the area on personal business.

It is usually not wise to interview people in the congregation and attempt to get evaluative information from them about the pastor. The risk is that you could either receive skewed perspective from an embittered person or confront a devoted member who would freak out if he thought you were there to lay claim to a beloved shepherd.

Should the pastor know that a delegation from your team is coming? Definitely! It avoids any possibility of getting there only to discover a different speaker. Yes, it may allow the pastor to prepare his best. But if he does not impress you at his best, then what he might have sounded like if you had not informed him doesn't really matter. Some teams choose to request a list of the Sundays within the span of a month that would be appropriate Sundays to visit. The specific date of the planned visit is not indicated, but you have provided the pastor opportunity to prepare his leadership team, if he chooses. You certainly do not want to create embarrassment for a pastor by popping in and causing his leadership team to wonder what is going on?

Scheduling a definite date with the candidate and his wife for your visit allows for a planned interview. If given a choice, opt to meet with the pastor in his residence so you can become acquainted with his family and observe his home.

Ascertain his level of interest in pastoring your church. Offer any additional information about your church and community. Inquire if the salary proposal sent earlier needs discussion or clarification -- or even negotiation. Be particularly sensitive to the housing preference -- private housing or church owned parsonage. Learn how soon he could relocate, if God led him to your church. Assure him that your team will be in prayer and discussion regarding his availability, and he will be notified of your decision following the next meeting.

**On a Practical Note:**

Establish guidelines for expenses and reimbursement before you visit a pastor onsite. Members of the team who visit a candidate onsite should be reimbursed for mileage (per mile), lodging, meals, and incidentals. As stated earlier in this book, you may want to include this in a Pastoral Discovery Team "budget."

## 8. Evaluate and Decide

If the visiting PDT members have had adequate time to compare evaluations and the full team senses agreement that this is "the man," he should be invited to candidate at a mutually suitable date. A man may prefer to come first as a pulpit supply so he can better determine his feelings about the church before becoming a candidate. You may also prefer it this way, feeling that a double exposure is better than a single visit.

While this may seem to be desirable, be aware of some disadvantages. If the distance is significant, this represents additional costs. You will also have to decide whether to defray the cost of bringing in his wife, if it is not a candidating occasion. Also, in this situation people would be evaluating only a man's pulpit ministry without due regard for his other pastoral skills, which would be considered if he were to be voted on as a candidate. Furthermore, most pastors would find it difficult to be away two Sundays within a short period. Generally, just one Sunday is used.

## 9. Narrowing It Down to One Candidate

The Pastoral Discovery Team bears a great burden as the procedure demands that out of several possibilities, one man must be chosen as the candidate, to visit the church, preach, meet the people and subsequently be voted on.

The procedure is simple but important.

- Time should be spent at that meeting for prayer. It might be helpful to announce to the congregation that the team will meet that week to make its final choice, asking for prayer on their behalf.

- Complete profiles should be prepared on all men containing:

- Material from associational headquarters,

- A résumé of recommendations from other sources

- Notes of the team's visit with the candidate

- His own reference questionnaire

- Before any discussion on the merits of the candidate is made, it might be helpful for each team member to rank the candidates independently.

- Following the ranking, as the member announces his first choice, he should give reasons why he has so chosen.

- It often happens that the ranking is unanimous. The task is then complete. If the ranking is not unanimous, the team must move on to agree on the one candidate for presentation to the church. It is well to remember that none are ideal but that the charge to the team is clear: "Select the candidate who comes closest to meeting your qualifications and make a firm decision regarding his candidacy."

## CONCLUSION

It should be noted that in many, if not most, cases the church will select the candidate that the team presents. This is vital to understand. In a way, the Pastoral Discovery Team *is* selecting the pastor. It is of paramount importance that the team brings to candidate only men who they would have as *their* pastor. If the team has been selected well and is truly a "cross-section" of the congregation, then this should be nothing but positive for the church.

## PASTORAL DISCOVERY TEAM- CHAPTER TEN *WORK IT OUT!*

List the nine points above and assign someone to each.

1. _____

2. _____

3. _____

4. _____

5. _____

6. _____

7. _____

8. _____

9. _____

List the ways you will apply the nine points of chapter ten to the process of selecting your prime candidate.

_____

_____

_____

_____

_____

What others needs and issues need to be considered at this point? _____

_____

Together, as a team, take time to thank the Lord for the one or two best candidates He has revealed to you. Pray especially for the single best candidate. Pray for the team members of the Pastoral Discovery Team that they will have the peace of God through this process.

# CHAPTER ELEVEN
## Presentation: The Candidating Process

Fewer things are more exciting than having a pastoral candidate presented to the church. After what may have been a devastating blow with the loss of the previous pastor, and following what sometimes can be "hard times" during the interim, it is a positive and hopeful step for a church to know that it "almost" has its next pastor.

Conversely, when a church "drops the ball" at this point and an otherwise hopeful candidate "walks away," it can be a very stressful and depressing time. That is why it is so important to handle the candidating process well. Here are some pointers.

## 1. Plan the Candidating Event

Carefully work out the schedule of activities for the candidate's visit. Invite his wife to accompany him, and his children, if feasible. Having the children present if they are very young may serve no valuable purpose. Older children usually would want to be part of the major decision they may face. It is understandable if they would like to see the community and schools.

Some churches prefer a Wednesday through Sunday visit; others have a weeklong candidating experience to enable the church to get to know the pastor better. The longer candidating enables members of the church family to set up personal appointments with the potential new spiritual leader.

Friday through Sunday seems to be the most popular format. Friday evening might be used as a public get-acquainted occasion, either at a dinner or a dessert setting. The candidate and his wife would be introduced and asked to give brief testimonies of their conversions. He could tell of his call to ministry and churches served. General questions of interest could be asked by the people present. Keep this to a reasonable length so that it does not drag on exhaustingly.

Saturday can be used for visiting the community, looking at potential housing or the parsonage and perhaps a meeting with combined boards and leaders. You might schedule your guests into two key homes for lunch and supper. Allow the couple to get a good night's rest for a strenuous Sunday.

If the visiting candidate is expected to teach a class in Sunday School, be sure to notify him of this assignment in adequate time to prepare. In order to observe his leadership in worship, request that he read the Scripture lesson and offer the pastoral prayer. If it is a communion Sunday, the deacons should preview with him the procedures and his part in them. Most candidates would prefer not to conduct the entire morning service in a new situation. Let him know how and when the service usually ends.

A Sunday afternoon meeting with the candidate may be used to cover any matters not yet discussed. If there is an evening service, the candidate usually is expected to preach again. He will be interested in knowing if it is less formal, held in a different room and if the style of ministry is usually more teaching-oriented.

## 2. Be Sensitive to the Candidate's Children

If the children accompany the visiting pastor, introduce them to the congregation but do not expect them to speak or to feel comfortable with much public exposure. This scrutiny is difficult for children. Let them stay in the background. Perhaps arrangements can be made for them to be cared for during any sessions that their parents need to attend on Saturday or Sunday afternoon.

## 3. Reserve Adequate Accommodations

Your special quests will appreciate being lodged in facilities that allow them privacy for personal discussions and rest. A good hotel room (or rooms) should be reserved for this occasion, if at all possible. It will create an impression of sensitivity and consideration. Be sure to make arrangements regarding the bill when you reserve the dates. Under no circumstances should the candidate find himself in an awkward situation where he is expected to pay the bill!

### 4. Publicize the Schedule

The candidating schedule should be announced at least two weeks in advance. (Check your constitution in this regard.) The date and time of the business meeting for extending a call may also be announced at the same time. In the publicity be sure to give a profile of the pastor, his family, training and churches served. The people need to know as much as possible about him.

### 5. Arrange for Reimbursement

All expenses and an honorarium should be paid to the candidate before he returns home. Arrange with the treasurer in advance for this check to be presented. This kind of thoughtfulness communicates your concern for the potential pastor's financial well-being. Never should the candidating weekend cost the candidate anything. Be as generous as possible. God will bless you for this.

### 6. Review the Weekend

Though a business meeting may have already been slated, the team needs to review the candidating event and determine a final "go" for the big vote. If something detected in the weekend's encounter is cause for alarm or if the team does not have consensus about proceeding, then the business meeting should be cancelled or used to give a report to the people. It is better to withdraw a recommendation then to proceed with misgivings. Your unanimous endorsement instills confidence with the people. They would not want to vote to call a candidate if there were reasons for the team's lack                    of                    confidence.

## 7. Avoid the "Tyranny of the One"

While it is desirable that the Pastoral Discovery Team has complete unanimity regarding the candidate, there are times when one person will "tyrannize" the rest of the team. What is meant by this is that if unanimity is "required" (not simply "desired"), one person can keep God's man from coming! This is a dangerous thing. There are a couple of ways to avoid this.

- Agree *ahead of time* that if there is only *one* dissension when the team votes, that the dissenting voter, recognizing that the Lord has moved in the heart of the team, will acquiesce to the rest of the team, so that there may be unanimity. If the Pastoral Discovery Team is larger (say, eight or nine), then do this if there are two dissenting votes.

- Strive for *consensus*, not unanimity. Consensus is an attitude that is adopted before the process begins. Simply put, every team member agrees that if the overwhelming majority of the team is in favor of a candidate, he or she will support the majority.

Let's face it; rarely will there be a time when a candidate is viewed as "perfect" by all the team. By acquiescing to the majority, or considering an overwhelming vote as consensus, each team member admits his or her own fallibility, and demonstrates a respect for the wisdom of the many.

This does *not* always mean that a dissenting vote is wrong. There are times when a "lone voter" is right about the candidate. The reputation of the dissenting voter, his or her reasons for voting "no," and information disclosed by the dissenting voter must all be considered. In the final analysis, however, a majority vote is the way congregationally governed churches operate. While it is preferable to have a unanimous vote, it is better to trust that God will reveal to at least the vast majority His will and direction regarding the candidate.

## CONCLUSION

The team may want to follow-up with the candidate before presenting him for church vote. There are times when the team is unanimous and the church is overwhelmingly excited, yet the candidate may, for whatever reasons, not want to come. It may be appropriate to call the candidate and ask him, after the intense candidating weekend, if he is still interested. A more pertinent question may be, "If we were to call you to be our pastor, will you accept?" Use discernment with such follow-up. It may be better to not ask the candidate such a question.

**PASTORAL DISCOVERY TEAM- CHAPTER ELEVEN *WORK IT OUT!***

Discuss and write down feedback about the seven points of chapter eleven.

1. _____

2. _____

3. _____

4. _____

5. _____

6. _____

7. _____

List the ways you will apply the principles of chapter eleven to the candidating weekend process:

_____

_____

_____

_____

_____

_____

What others needs and issues need to be considered at this point? _____

_____

Together, as a team, take time to thank the Lord for the candidating weekend, and ask Him to give the team unanimity concerning the candidate. Pray for the candidate and his family, and ask God to give Him discernment that is in keeping with what God has given your team. Pray that the Pastoral Discovery Team will have the peace of God through this process.

# CHAPTER TWELVE
## Remuneration: Compiling a Compensation Package

Pastoral compensation is probably the most controversial topic regarding the search process. "Money" is a touchy subject, to say the least, and if not handled properly, can be a source of contention and even dissension. Before we get into the process of developing a package for your next pastor, let's consider some mistakes churches make about pastoral remuneration.

## Mistakes with Pastoral Remuneration

Many church members do not like to think about this, but more often than not many mistakes are made concerning "taking care of the pastor." I speak as both a former layperson and a pastor (four different congregations) Here are just a few mistakes churches make (I hope you will avoid them).

1. Treating the pastor's pay like someone else's

   Many laypeople who plan the pastor's pay package think in terms of "their" pay package. For instance, if the pastor is receiving three weeks paid vacation, a layperson may say, "I do not get three weeks of vacation!" Or when dealing with a car allowance he may reason that he does not get a car allowance. This is not the point. The pastor's vocation is unique and causes him to incur unique expenses. We wouldn't compare doctors' pay to teachers' pay, or a forklift driver's pay to the CEO of the forklift company. It doesn't make sense to compare the pastor's pay with anyone else except other pastors with similar qualifications and in similar situations.

2. Claiming that the church "cannot afford it"

   This is an often-used excuse for not taking proper care of the pastor. As with household budgets, we can usually "afford" what we really want and place a high priority on. I have never seen a church that steps out on faith and takes good care of their pastor ever fall "short" of paying their pastor and taking care of the church's other expenses. The exception to this rule may be pastors who have asked for a truly unreasonable pay package.

3. Failing to realize the difference between "blue collar" and "white collar"

This is probably controversial, but there is a difference between the way blue collar folks and white collar folks "see" things. With that said, the pastoral position, by any means of the distinction, is a "white collar" vocation. Even pastors who pastor blue collar churches are themselves white collar. The exception to this may be some bi-vocational pastors, especially those in rural areas or in factory communities.

Why is this distinction important? The pastor's vocation requires some consideration that the blue collar worker may not think about. The pastor needs an auto allowance, because he does much of his work in his car. He needs books, which are the "tools" of his trade. He must continually study, and often must attain "continued education units" (CEU's). Often, especially in conservative churches in conservative communities , the pastor needs to have dress clothes for daily use. Keep in mind, too, that the pastor is technically "self-employed," and requires different retirement planning, tax considerations, etc. than those who work for a company.

We could list more under this category, but you get the picture. The important thing is that the pastor is treated fairly in light of his personal and vocational needs.

4. Failing to consider the pastor's education, experience, roles and responsibilities

Most vocations "reward" a person for continuing his or her education. The typical pastor has had seven to eight years of school after high school (a Master of Divinity, or M.Div.). Many have doctoral degrees. Additionally, the pastor's experience at previous churches needs to be considered, just as people in other white collar vocations are paid based on experience. Keep in mind, too, the roles and responsibilities of the pastor. He is a "professional counselor," a "fundraiser," an "administrator," a "public speaker," and a "manager."

Allow me to present one idea here that has helped many churches "attitudinally" adjust to these concepts. When you call a new pastor, treat him as if he has "transferred within the company." The "company" he works for is the "Body of Christ." His "CEO" (his "boss") is God. God determines where he will work "within the company." View your church as one "site" or "location" within the "company." This way it is easier to understand that, when your pastor arrives, he should be paid, at a minimum, what he was paid in his previous church (and generally more). Since he is "transferring" to your location, make sure that you maintain or increase his vacation package. You get the idea.

5. Accusing pastors of being in the ministry for the money

While I have heard this statement used many times, I have never known a pastor who was in the ministry "for the money." I have not even met one. If a man was in his vocation "for the money" he would not have gone into the ministry. Based on the education requirements, roles and responsibilities (see above), and emotional and mental stress that "goes with the territory," a gifted pastor could make a whole lot more money in the secular industry. Rest assured that your next pastor is surely not in the ministry "for the money."

6. Making the pastoral pay package a lower priority than it should be

Study the New Testament and you will see that God places a high value on how a church compensates its pastor. Your pastor's "package" should be more important than your facilities, programs, and savings account. It's that simple.

7. Making the pastor feel "guilty" for his pay package

Be generous with your new pastor. Give him "double honor." Be proud (in a good way) of how your church "takes care of" your pastor. Never, intentionally or inadvertently, make your pastor feel "guilty" about his remuneration. This violates scripture. You are to create an environment and a remuneration package that helps the pastor do his work with joy.

8. Presenting or determining the pastoral pay package in a business meeting setting

Churches are discovering more and more that the pastor's pay package should be discussed by and determined by a smaller group of people, and not the whole congregation. Can you imagine the guy at the office or the man at the factory having his pay discussed by the whole department? See points 3 and 4 above.

When your pastor's package is discussed publicly, it is awkward and embarrassing for him and his family. Also, some will be upset because the pastor "makes too little," and some will be jealous because they think he "makes too much."

For the sake of your church, the pastor and his family, keep these decisions at a board or team level. This may require a constitutional change, but it is well worth it. I have yet to meet a church that switched to this protocol that regretted it.

When you report salaries to your congregation, simply "lump" all salaries together (pastor, staff, secretary, custodian, etc.). This way everyone knows what is going out in compensation, but they do not know the "details" that will simply cause conflict. If your pastor is the only paid staff person, this may require reporting what he makes, but at least list his salary, housing, and benefits separately. Church leaders should emphasize that the "salary" is really what the pastor actually "makes."

9. Viewing the church as "hiring" a pastor instead of "calling" him

You never want to see yourself as "hiring" a pastor. Even in scriptural metaphorical language, the pastor (shepherd) is not to be a "hireling." Rather, view yourself as "calling" a pastor. This is in better keeping with the New Testament, and helps you to attitudinally treat the pastor as God's man, which he is.

I could list other mistakes churches make in this area, but these should be sufficient for getting your team working in the direction of generosity and courtesy when dealing with such a touchy subject.

## Who Should Develop the Pastoral Remuneration Package?

It may be a good idea that another team be formed to deal with this area. There is no doubt that in the American church the pastoral compensation package is controversial, and often divisive. I once talked with a pastor who had four families leave his church because he got a decent raise. "That money could have gone to missions," they said. There are several reasons for the Pastoral Discovery Team (PDT) to delegate this process to another team.

1. "Money" issues may cloud the judgment of the PDT. You may find yourself tempted to reject the best candidate because you cannot come to consensus regarding the pay package.

2. Keeping the two issues (the "call" and the "pay") separate helps the PDT to focus on the qualifications and suitableness of the candidate.

3. Because of the IRS codes, limitations of the church, and the changing climate of pastoral remuneration, the compensation process is complicated. The PDT has enough to do.

4. Finally, "money" issues often result in "power plays." The PDT does not need to be distracted with conflict and controversy over the potential pastor's pay package.

Whoever puts the pastoral compensation package together should follow the basic guidelines for remuneration below.

## Components of the Pastoral Compensation Package

The pastor's compensation plan (his "package") should be itemized under at least three categories: pastor's *income* (salary, housing and utility allowances), *business expenses* (auto expense, conference and continuing education expense), and *fringe benefits* (health insurance, retirement, etc.).

### 1. Pastor's Income

The pastor's "income" is what he actually "gets paid." This is an important distinction to make. Some laypeople will speak of their pastor's generous salary when in reality they are referring to his "package." The "income" is what the pastor immediately benefits from. There are essentially two parts to the pastor's income: salary; and housing and utilities.

## a. Salary

Hugh O. Chamliss says that there are some important factors a Church should consider when setting their pastor's salary:

- *A pastor's financial needs are the same as those of any other person. While his calling is unique, a pastor's physical, mental, and emotional needs are no different from those of any man.*

- *The salary of the pastor should be systematically and objectively set in order to be fair to him and his family, as well as to the church.*

- *A church should remember that a pastor incurs certain legitimate expenses in fulfilling his service responsibility to God and the church. These expenses should not be considered part of his salary but should be accurately reflected in the format of the budget.*

- *Other ministers' salaries can be poor guides in setting the pastor's salary. Pastors' salaries in general are usually below the community average.*

- *Annual adjustments should be made in the pastor's salary and church pastoral expenses to reflect variations in the cost of living merit increases, and other changing expenses.*

"Two medians can help the church solve the pay puzzle," says Glenn Arnold in the January 1974 issue of Moody Monthly: "the 'community medians' and the 'congregational medians'."

- The community median is found through examining the school board salary scales and Chamber of Commerce median income information for the community. I would like to add that median incomes are now readily available on the internet. Concludes Arnold: "If a pastor is to function actively, positively and efficiently in his community, he will need to be salaried on or near the community median."

- Asking the church board members to list their personal annual salaries—unsigned—can give a median congregational income. Arnold further states, "Many local church leaders and denominational officers believe that the pastor's salary should fall in the higher section of the congregational middle income range." And Hugh Chambliss, [past] Superintendent of Missions for a Southern Baptist Association in Alabama, says: "The church should designate in its budget an amount for the pastor at least equal to or above the average professional male church member." All of this, of course, presupposes that the church is calling a well-trained and experienced pastor.

It should also be noted that pastors pay their own social security as self-employed persons. In business and industry this cost is shared by the employer. The church cannot pay this by withholding, but it can allow an additional amount in the form of salary and the pastor can pay it himself.

Some churches clearly cannot afford to pay what ought to be paid in salaries and benefits. Students, coming out of seminary, because of lack of experience cannot command such a salary. Men nearing retirement often find this to be true also.

When a church finds itself unable to meet even a minimum salary and benefits it has several alternatives:

- To call a pastor who is in retirement who wishes to continue to minister

- To call a pastor who is willing to earn his livelihood by serving the Church part time and working at other work part time (referred to as "bi-vocayional"). A careful Agreement as to the time expected of him should be worked out in advance of the call.

- To share a pastor with another church or institution, working in a yoke- arrangement with another association or Baptist church or school or institution in the area. While this is not always ideal, it still spells the difference between having a ministry and not having one.

- To call a layman, licensed to preach, who earns his livelihood through some other means. This may be the shape of the future for many small country churches and inner-city churches.

### b. Housing and Utility Allowance

Very few churches provide parsonages anymore, but since some still do I include it here. Should the church pay a housing allowance or provide a parsonage for the pastor? There are pros and cons on the subject. We must not overlook the fact that a church-owned parsonage or manse is an arrangement that exists *primarily as a convenience to the congregation,* not to the pastor. This is why the minister does not have to pay federal income tax on the value of his housing. Traditionally, the arrangement has been the result of the congregation's desire to have a resident minister.

More and more, however, especially in urban and suburban areas, pastors are choosing a housing allowance to own their home because of a number of benefits they feel strongly about:

- **Independence**. This is true even though he uses the housing allowance to rent a home. "This is our own home." They have chosen it to fit *their* needs and tastes.

- **Security**. They feel they are making an investment in their financial future by building equity in a house especially in the inflationary trend of this era.

- **Stability**. Pastors tend to sink their roots into the community.

On the other hand, there are some cons about this matter of home ownership – some of which few pastors foresee:

- Mobility is reduced. It is more difficult to move, simply because of the logistics of selling, etc. and in a down market the Lord may hardly lead the man to another place.

- It is possible to lose a substantial amount on a declining market or if a man stays only a few years and builds little or no equity.

- Since most pastors have not been able to save very much and have few investments, the problem of the substantial down payment is real. Some churches make possible a low-interest loan reserve, kept always for that purpose. His loan need not be paid until he leaves and the house is sold. (Some states however, prohibit by law borrowing the down payment on a house.)

- While there is an unspoken suggestion of freedom in the offer of a housing allowance, the pastor is not as free as it may seem to live where he wants to live. He will often be expected to live where the majority of his congregation lives, whether he likes it or not.

- Often the housing allowance paid by the church is less than the cost of owning a home. Horace O. Duke, in a past issue of *Church Administration* magazine, stated:

*"An important factor in the consideration of a housing allowance is who is really paying for it. Many pastors actually take a cut in total compensation by changing from a parsonage arrangement to a housing allowance plan. The housing allowance is often a cheaper arrangement but it can be a more costly one for the pastor. A pastor living in a parsonage may receive hidden benefits, which should be taken into account in setting the amount of his housing allowance. These include utilities, phone, insurance, taxes and repairs. These*

*would normally be an unnoticed part of the church's cost in providing a pastor with a parsonage."*

A pastor, after understanding all of the facts, ought to be allowed the option to purchase his own home. It goes without saying that adequate housing allowance ought therefore to be budgeted. Chambliss gives helpful insight to the Pastoral Discovery Team:

*"If a house is provided for the pastor, the worth of the house or its cost to the church should not be deducted from the pastor's income, since he does not own it and will have no equity in it after he ceases to live in it. If an amount is to be deducted, a fair amount would be one equal to the interest value and utilities furnished. These he would not expect to recover if it were his house and he sold it. Since he could at least expect to recover the principal value if he owned the house, that amount should be a part of his salary if a house owned by the church is furnished by him. Many churches now furnish a home allowance in lieu of furnishing a house. If this is done, the amount should be sufficient to make payments and to provide utilities and upkeep. This allowance should be part of his salary if the salary has been fairly set. House allowances are not reported as taxable income. In addition, the interest is tax deductible. In many cases, it is best for the pastor and the church is an allowance is provided as part of the pastor's salary, but it must be so indicated in the budget."*

Here is another thought if your pastor must live in a parsonage. Let the pastor and his wife choose the decorations (carpet, paint, wallpaper, etc.) and have these done before he moves in the parsonage. If possible, this should be paid for by the church (he does not get to keep the house, nor will he get any financial return from these improvements- the church does). It is a sweet and generous act, especially for the pastor's wife, when they are allowed to decorate according to their tastes.

c. **Equity Allowance**

There is an alternative for churches with parsonages that allows them to still offer their pastor "equity." This is called the "equity allowance."

Pastors who are buying their homes know how much equity means for the future. The pastor who lives in a parsonage has no such security. Why not start a savings plan in which the church puts the equivalent of the annual equity of the parsonage (simply have your banker or CPA estimate what the equity would be on the parsonage if the pastor were buying it). The parsonage is mainly, after all, a benefit to the church. It is rarely financially beneficial to the pastor. Contrary to popular belief, it is not "free" housing. In the long run, the pastor will pay dearly. Take care of God's man in this area.

I attended a tax-seminar at which the speaker stated that the typical pastor who lives in a parsonage his entire ministry loses a half million dollars during that time. It is something to think about.

Remember that the church always has the principle value of the parsonage, and rarely will an equity allowance equal the actual full equity of the house. Keep in mind that the parsonage is part of your pastor's compensation. It is not free housing. He is "earning" it. He is, in essence, paying for it.

According to H.B. London, Jr. (previously of *Focus on the Family*), pastors who are allowed to buy their own homes stay longer! If your church has high pastoral turnover, and you have a parsonage, this is something to think about. In my consulting with pastors, equity is a priority item. Every church who gives two hoots about their pastor should evaluate where they are on the housing issue.

## 2. Business Expense

Another much-misunderstood area of pastoral remuneration is the business expense allowance. In reality, this is not *remuneration* but *reimbursement*. In other words, these monies do not benefit the pastor *personally*. There are several categories under the broad heading of "business expenses."

### a. Auto Expense

There are essentially three ways to treat the auto allowance: 1) pay the pastor nothing for auto expenses, forcing him to absorb the expenses himself (which makes his "pay" substantially lower); 2) reimburse the pastor for professionally incurred auto expenses; and 3) provide the pastor with a car (or other vehicle).

- **No Auto Allowance**

  While this seems like an obviously unfair approach, the pastor may willingly opt for this if his pay package is inordinately high. This, however, is rarely the case. In most cases, the pastor simply cannot afford to "absorb" the costs of professionally incurred auto expenses. Using the example below, the pastor would "lose" over $3,900 per year with this arrangement. Look at it this way; if your church goes this route, it has essentially "cut" the pastor's pay by $3,900.

- **Auto Expense Reimbursement**

This is by far the most common way to treat the auto allowance. At the time of this writing the IRS allows a set amount per mile for the first so many miles and a smaller portion per mile for additional mileage. Research shows that pastors drive as many as 15,000 miles a year for church work. For illustrational purposes, let's assume your pastor drives about 150 miles a week, or 7,800 miles per year, for church-related work (home visitation, meetings, hospital visits, training sessions, etc.). Choosing an allowance that reflects this would appear to be fair. For example, if the IRS's going rate is 50 cents per mile for the first 12,000 miles, based on a 7,800 per year usage, the car allowance will look like this: $.50 x 7,800 = $3,900. Some churches pay mileage only, which is most fair, but often the occasion for misunderstanding. If a pastor drives sixty miles to a neighboring city to visit a parishioner who is to have serious surgery and his wife goes along and they spend three hours shopping, was it a business trip or pleasure? Should the pastor pay part of the tab? Because of the possible misunderstandings, we suggest a flat amount. It would seem that even small churches ought to recognize the need for a minimum payment (of some fair dollar amount) per year. In no way should the auto expense amount of the budget be considered salary, since in fact most pastors subsidize the work of the church through the auto costs they absorb themselves.

- **Provide the Pastor with a Car**

  This may seem a little extravagant at first, but when you consider that a church may reimburse a pastor $5,000 or more a year for auto expenses, it may make sense to simply provide him with an automobile. This vehicle (to be picked by the pastor) is "owned" by the church. It is in the church's name and under the church's insurance plan. The church should "maintain" the car and give the pastor a gasoline credit card (or charge card) so that he may purchase gas for business use. If the pastor uses the vehicle for personal use, he simply reports that and pays the appropriate taxes to the IRS. While this arrangement is not as common as auto expense reimbursement, it is becoming increasingly popular. Check out the guidelines for this plan with your accountant and the IRS regulations.

Regardless of which auto-expense plan you choose, determine ahead of time not to hold the pastor hostage with it. In other words, don't allow your generosity now to become a bone of contention later.

b. **Conference Expenses**

An allowance for conventions and conferences will permit spiritual renewal for the pastor. The church benefits greatly. Travel costs, hotel room costs, and per diem food allowances should be budgeted, plus registration fees. Some churches prefer to pay actual costs. When the conference is a great distance away the cost of air travel should be allowed regardless of the mode of travel he elects to use. If the pastor should choose to drive, additional travel time other than a day at each end should then be considered vacation time.

## c. Continuing Education Expenses

More and more churches are budgeting a modest amount to pay for short seminars, etc. now that so much is available for excellence in the ministry. The value to the church is immense.

## d. Hospitality Allowance

Many pastors easily spend $1,000 or more per year out-of-pocket for entertaining guests on behalf of the church. To make some provision in the budget, however small, says that the church takes note of this expense and it is grateful for the ministry. Keep in mind that the pastor often entertains other ministers, including guests, missionaries, and laypeople.

## e. Office Expenses

Pastors today need a lot of office equipment that previous generations of pastors did not have. Your pastor uses email, software, electronic commentaries, online services (some requiring prescriptions), smart phones, etc. All of these items cost money, and he generally uses them almost exclusively for church work. Why not buy him a laptop computer or I-Pad (or split the costs) and make sure he has all the "tools" necessary to function in a technological age? Stamps, letterhead, thank you cards, etc. should be paid for by the church (except for the pastor's "personal" use).

### f. Other Business Expenses

There may be other business expenses incurred by the pastor. These should be addressed before the new pastor arrives, or as soon as he discloses them to you. The "rule of thumb" is, if the expense is incurred for the church's benefit and as part of the pastor's job, the church should reimburse him for it.

## 3. Fringe Benefits

The pastor, like those in all modern vocations, should receive some "fringe benefits" that will help him better provide for the long-term care of his family. Some of these benefits are:

### a. Health and Life Insurance and Related Products

- Life Insurance Benefits

- Accidental Death and Dismemberment Benefits

- Long Term Disability Income Benefit

- Educational Benefits

- Hospital Benefits

- Surgical Benefits

- Maternity Benefits

- In-Hospital Doctor's Calls

- Major Medical Benefits

### b. A Retirement Plan

There was a time when a pastor never thought of retiring. Many think that it is because the pastors of the past were more "godly" than those now. In reality, many never retired because they couldn't! That does not have to be. The church should be sure there is a retirement account that they and the pastor contribute to.

### c. Adequate Vacation Time

Most specialists today agree that the typical pastor should receive at least four weeks of paid vacation. While this is actually part of the pastor's "salary," it is viewed as a "fringe benefit" because the pastor is receiving money for time he did not work. This is the same with all vocations. The special demands on pastors, as well as their needs to be constantly spiritually and physically vibrant, present them with the special need for occasional rest. Your package should not only state a starting vacation allowance, but it should state how the pastor can (or cannot) accumulate additional vacation days or weeks. The most common is to add an extra week for every five years of service.

### d. A Scheduled Lengthy Sabbatical

This used to be common for ministers in a bygone era, but today few pastors receive sabbaticals. The reason is that too many churches view sabbaticals as "free long vacations." Your pastor should receive a three-to-six month sabbatical about every seven years. While such sabbaticals can be logistical nightmares, the effort is well worth it for the pastor and the church. The seven-year threshold should be trans-ministry. That is, the pastor should receive such a sabbatical every seven years, regardless of the tenure in your church. For example, if you call a pastor who has not had a sabbatical in four years, you may offer him one at the end of his third year with you. If he is arriving at your church after a full seven years without sabbatical, you may want to wait a year or two to offer him one, or provide one for him before he arrives. It is a given that only churches with certain staff and financial resources can pull this off. The rule of thumb is: if you can, than you should.

e.  Other Fringe Benefits

If other fringe benefits are suggested or considered, try to deal with these before the new pastor arrives. As with the salary and other benefits, it is best that a team or a board deal with these, and not the congregation.

*A Word of Challenge*: Church members may cringe at the list of policies and the amounts for the business expense and fringe benefits. However, these are real costs. Someone is paying for them. On the basis of fairness and on the basis of the Word of God, "And let the one who is taught the Word share all good things with him who teaches" (Galatians 6), a church should seek to do its very best in all these areas. A pastor who is not preoccupied with dire financial needs is a man who can get on with the business of the ministry!

Smaller churches, of course, have less to work with, but efforts toward providing these must continually be made. Explanations to the prospective pastor and full disclosure of church finances will help him have a clearer understanding of the situation and determine his acceptance of the call.

It may be pointed out that all of these matters may need to be negotiated with the candidate during his candidation visit to the church.

## CONCLUSION

The length of this chapter and the complexity of the issues should give you some idea as to why it may be best that a whole other team deal with pastoral remuneration. Give this section your best shot! If you are calling a man who will make a difference in your church and your lives, surely you want to give him "double honor."

**PASTORAL DISCOVERY TEAM- CHAPTER TWELVE *WORK IT OUT!***

Discuss and write down feedback about the three main points of chapter twelve.

1. _____

    _____

2. _____

    _____

3. _____

    _____

Who should determine the pastoral compensation package and why?

_____

_____

_____

_____

_____

_____

What others needs and issues need to be considered at this point? _____

_____

_____

Together, as a team, take time to thank the Lord for the fact that He wants you to care for your next pastor. Ask Him to give the team unanimity concerning the pastoral compensation process. Pray for the candidate and his family, and ask God to give Him discernment that is in keeping with what God has given your team. Pray that the Pastoral Discovery Team will have the peace of God through this process.

## CHAPTER THIRTEEN
## Invitation: Extending a Call to Your New Pastor

Assuming that the candidating weekend went well, and that the details of the call have been worked out with and agreed upon by the candidate, it is now time to proceed to extending a call to the candidate. This is an exciting time that has been much-anticipated! Don't drop the ball here; handle it well.

### 1. Schedule the Business Meeting

The business meeting at which the church "votes" for the candidate should be conducted as soon as possible. Everyone, including the candidate, is anxious to know what the action of the church will be. Often the business session is held on the Sunday night the man candidates and after he has left. If this is planned, the team needs to do its final review prior to the evening service. Some churches prefer to make the decision the following Wednesday night, which allows some time for reflection and interaction among the church family. Still others feel that the next Sunday morning, after the service, is best because of maximum participation in the decision process. It is not the best procedure to vote on the candidate after the morning service at which he preaches, unless the church is very small and there is no evening service.

### 2. Consult Your Constitution

Determine how the business session is to be conducted and who is to moderate it. Find out from your constitution what number constitutes a quorum. Be clear about the percentage of votes required to extend a call and the age requirements for voting. If there is a time element attached to this procedure, obey it completely. For instance, if your constitution states that the vote for a pastor must be announced in the pulpit two weeks in advance, determine if this means two "Sunday services" or two actual "weeks." The key is to appease even the most avid "constitution follower." You don't want a "technicality" to come back to haunt you.

Also be sure that you understand the constitution's requirement for the percentage of the vote necessary to call a pastor. In most cases it will be a minimum of 75% positive votes of those present. Additionally, the candidate should have a set percentage in his mind that he is comfortable with. For example, he may feel that even though he can be called with a 75% vote, he prefers to have at least 90% affirmative. This is important to know in advance. Nothing would be more disappointing than to call a candidate, say at 77%, to only learn later that he will not come with a vote less than 90%. The candidate should be aware of any constitution requirements regarding the voting process.

## 3. Conduct the Business

Begin the business meeting with prayer. The Pastoral Discover team chairperson should state the unanimous (or overwhelming consensus) recommendation of the team and move that the attending members vote to invite the candidate to become pastor, with the terms clearly indicated. This is usually termed "the call." This is actually an acknowledging of what a church senses may be God's call to a man to come and serve as pastor.

The motion should be seconded and then discussion allowed. A vote should be a secret ballot so as not to pressure conformity to the will of the majority or of the leadership. The vote should be taken in accordance with the stipulations of your constitution regarding eligibility for voting and percentage of vote needed to issue an official call. Be sure that people understand how to mark their ballots. "Yes" indicates a vote to call the candidate; "No" is a vote not to issue a call. "Abstention" should be written on the ballot by those who choose not to register a vote. Make certain that pencils are available for marking the ballots and that clerks are appointed to tally and report the result, including any abstentions.

## 4. Seek United Support

If the tally of the ballots is sufficient for a call to be extended, but there are some negative votes, ask if there can be a unanimous vote of support if the man accepts the call. This may be done by raising hands or standing. This assures the man being invited to shepherd the church that all expressed willingness to cooperate with him and support the majority decision. The chairperson of the meeting should announce that the pastor will be contacted promptly and given the results of the vote.

Appreciation should be expressed to the PDT. It may be appropriate to give them a gift at the end of the meeting. Gift certificates to a nearby restaurant or some other modest token of appreciation will say a lot about the church's appreciation of the hard work done by the team. A motion to adjourn the business session should be moved, seconded and passed.

## 5. Notify the Candidate

The candidate should be notified by phone of the vote promptly. His decision as to accept the call or not should be asked for at that time. If he requests time to consider the matter, ask him to notify you within a week, preferably in time to announce it at the next service. If the motion did not carry to call the pastor, let him know the vote as graciously as possible and thank him for his availability and prayer. Never convey a negative vote by mail. It is better that the team chairperson (or his or her designee) calls the candidate and inform him of the results. Be sure to be as sensitive as possible.

## 6. Mail or Email Official Terms

The official action of the church and the terms of the call, including all financial and living arrangements, should be mailed or emailed quickly to the pastor. (See sample "Terms of the Call" in Appendix 4). This becomes a binding agreement and it should be absolutely clear.

## 7. Announce the Good News!

As soon as the candidate has indicated his acceptance of the call, release the happy news to the congregation and to the community. An arrival time should be announced. Give this to your local newspaper for a write-up. Be sure, too, to promptly notify your regional association office.

## 8. Get Ready for the Big Day

See the next chapter to help you prepare for the arrival of your new pastor and his family!

## CONCLUSION

While the pastoral discovery process is a lengthy and difficult journey, the pay-off is well worth the investment. If the team has handled the process well, and the church has entered into the calling procedures saturated in prayer and unity, it is almost certain that they will succeed in calling the man *God* wants for their church! Praise Him above all names!

**PASTORAL DISCOVERY TEAM- CHAPTER THIRTEEN *WORK IT OUT!***

Discuss and write down feedback and strategies for the first seven points of chapter thirteen.

1. _____

2. _____

3. _____

4. _____

5. _____

6. _____

7. _____

List the ways you will apply the principles of chapter thirteen to the calling process:

_____

_____

_____

_____

_____

_____

What others needs and issues need to be considered at this point? _____

Together, as a team, take time to thank the Lord for the candidate He has brought your way, and ask Him to give the church unanimity (or overwhelming consensus) concerning the calling of the candidate. Pray for the candidate and his family, and ask God to give Him discernment that is in keeping with what God has given your church. Pray that the Pastoral Discovery Team and the church will have the peace of God through this process.

# CHAPTER FOURTEEN
## Disintegration: Dissolving the Pastoral Discovery Team

The Pastoral Discover Team (or Pulpit Committee or Pastoral Search Committee) should not be a "standing" committee. There comes a time to dissolve and disband this team, and here is the time. It is important that the PDT is dissolved *before* the pastor arrives. This brief chapter offers a few suggestions for this process.

- Upon hearing a positive reply from the candidate, the final meeting of the Pastoral Discover Team (PDT) is held. Make this an affirming meeting, and celebrate what God has done through the team! There is much to be glad about!

- Plans should be made for the installation service (see Chapter Sixteen). If this becomes the task of the church board, the PDT should have some relationship to those plans. This should be established in advance to avoid "territorialism" and disappointment.

- A report of the acceptance should be made formally to the church. This is offered by the PDT chairperson or his or her designee.

- Pictures and a news story should be provided for the local newspaper. Generally the newspaper will carry its full story on the first Sunday the pastor preaches.

- Destroy or return all confidential papers concerning prospective candidates.

- Send "Thank you" letters or emails to all men who were nominees for the candidacy. This will also serve to notify them they are no longer under consideration. Christian courtesy demands this, yet so many churches neglect it. Please be gracious!

- A brief summary report of the team's work should be submitted for inclusion in the church clerk's records.

- A full accounting of expenses should be presented to the treasurer and any unpaid bills presented for payment.

- With the final report to the church, the team should be formally discharged as a task force or committee—with thanks.

## CONCLUSION

As a member of the PDT, you are a valuable asset to the church and a genuine servant of the Lord. Be pleased in your heart to know that you have served in such an important capacity.

## PASTORAL DISCOVERY TEAM-
## CHAPTER FOURTEEN *WORK IT OUT!*

Discuss and assign who will do the various follow-up mentioned in this chapter. Write down feedback and strategies for the main points of chapter fourteen.

1. _____

2. _____

3. _____

4. _____

5. _____

6. _____

7. _____

List any other ways you will accomplish the steps in chapter fourteen for dissolving the PDT:

_____

_____

_____

_____

_____

_____

What others needs and issues need to be considered at this point? _____

_____

Together, as a team, take time to thank the Lord for the opportunity He has brought your way, and ask Him to give you a sense of satisfaction regarding the role you played at this juncture of your church's history. Affirm each other and conclude well.

## CHAPTER FIFTEEN
## Celebration: How to Welcome Your New Pastor

Now that all the "hard work" is over, it's now time to do some more hard work! Welcoming your new pastor and his family requires a lot of foresight, teamwork, and intentionality. Be sure to give this process the effort it deserves.

Since the Pastoral Discovery Team (PDT) will be dissolved by this point, the PDT may want to formulate a plan and delegate it to another team (either appointed by the PDT or by the church board), or the PDT may work together (if acceptable by the board and the church) as a Pastoral Welcome Team after the PDT has been officially disbanded. You do not want to welcome your new pastor with the words, "Welcome, I am on the pastoral search committee." It is better to say, "Welcome from the Pastoral Welcome Team!"

### 1. Plan His Moving

There are essentially four ways to handle a pastor's relocation to your church: 1) let him handle the process of "from there to here" totally from his end; 2) let him handle his end (departure) and you handle your end (arrival); 3) you handle the process of "from there to here" totally from your end; and 4) a professional moving company is hired and does a turnkey move. The turnkey move is obviously the best for everyone, so I will deal with that one first, then the other three will be covered.

a. Professional "Turnkey" Movers

The best way to move a pastor is by professional movers. If your church can afford this, it is the best way for everyone. I have yet to talk to a pastor who does not agree with this. The move is trying enough as it is without the pastor having to do it all himself, so this approach will be much-appreciated and easier on all involved. A professional mover will literally pack and label the boxes, carefully move the furniture and belongings, replace damaged items, and unload all said items at the pastor's new home. Here are some guidelines to follow:

- Allow the pastor to choose the moving company

  Since the move begins on "his end," it is best to allow the pastor to choose who will move him. He will want to consult with the church board, of course, and he will certainly keep the price in mind. The important thing is that he is allowed to get the best mover he is comfortable with.

- Don't be stingy with the price.

  While you do not want to "overspend" on a mover, neither do you want to be a tightwad. Work out a price with the mover. Be sure that this will not be an issue later when the "bill arrives."

- Pay for the mover directly rather than by reimbursement to the pastor.

  While movers are well-worth the investment, they are expensive; there is no doubt about it. It will be very difficult for most pastors to come up with the thousands of dollars necessary to pay a professional mover. It is far better that the church, who is going to pay for the movers anyway, to pay the movers directly. Most moving companies will be glad to have this arrangement.

- Make the pastor "feel good" about getting to choose this option.

  It may be tempting by some to "offer" the pastor this option, but to inadvertently (or purposefully) make him feel "guilty" about it. There are several reasons someone might do this (i.e. they hope he will decline the professional mover, they want to make him feel the church is really "sacrificing," etc.). It is very important that whoever works with the pastor on the church end to be very positive and upbeat about this expenditure. Let the pastor know you are genuinely glad to do this.

- Pay all related expenses (unless another agreement has been made ahead of time.

  As mentioned earlier, the professional mover should be paid for by the church. There may be other related expenses to move. Please be sure to communicate with the pastor concerning this, and unless it is some extravagant and unnecessary expenditure (which the pastor should pay for), you should cover these bills also.

b. The Pastor "Does It All"

This is the least desirable approach. Here the pastor arranges the U-Haul, the packing and unpacking, the loading and unloading, etc. Please do not allow this to happen. If this does happen, it is imperative that the church pays all the bills related to the move. To do otherwise is unthinkable.

c. The Pastor and Church "Share the Load"

This may be a necessary route for smaller churches. In this approach the pastor takes care of his end (packing and loading) and the church takes care of him on their end (unloading and unpacking). He will generally get volunteers from his old church or other friends to help him get packed, and you will have volunteers from your church unload and unpack him at his arrival. In many cases the men (and stronger women!) will unload the U-Haul and the ladies (and weaker men?) will unpack boxes, etc.). As with all the methods, be sure to pay for all related expenses.

d. The Church "Does It All"

If your church simply cannot afford a professional mover, this is the next-best option. Here is a simple outline of what to do:

- Arrange for a U-Haul and other vehicles to move the pastor's "stuff"

- Arrange for volunteers to go to the pastor's current home and help him and his wife pack and load their belongings (this may require a night over)

- Treat the pastor's "stuff" with respect and courtesy. If things are broken, replace them, etc.

- Have another group of volunteers "waiting" for the pastor when he arrives. They will unload and unpack

- In many cases the men (and stronger women!) will unload the U-Haul and the ladies (and weaker men?) will unpack boxes, etc.

- As with all the methods, be sure to pay for all related expenses.

Careful planning and execution of the moving process will serve as the positive first step in what you hope will be a long and blessed relationship with your new shepherd.

## 2. Prepare the Parsonage

If your church has a parsonage, make sure everything is ready for the pastor's family. Any fixing up, painting or cleaning should be cared for so that you are proud to turn over the home to your new pastor and family. As mentioned before, if possible allow the pastor and his wife to choose wallpaper, paint colors, etc. in advance and have this work done before they arrive.

## 3. Hold a Food Shower

An old-fashioned custom that is still very much in order is to stock the cupboards with food prior to the pastor's arrival. A week or two of contributing food items can be a great welcome treat for the new family who has probably depleted their pantry prior to moving. If the pastor is buying or renting his own home, arrange for a Food Shower shortly after his arrival.

## 4. Arrange Arrival Help

It is very thoughtful to send dinner to the pastor's house for their first evening (or several evenings) in their new home. Child care during unloading might also be most helpful. Perhaps assistance with making beds and settling essentials for the first night would be appreciated, too.

## 5. Give the Pastor Time to "Move In"

Give him time to move in, become acquainted with the area, register children in school, register for driver's license, voting, etc. Do not deluge him with speaking invitations the first weeks.

## 6. Schedule an Installation

It is customary and meaningful for the church to host an installation service as soon after arrival as possible. It probably ought to be planned prior to arrival and in consultation with the pastor-elect. Since it is appropriate to invite neighboring pastors and churches to attend, it usually is help on a Sunday afternoon or weekday evening. Several nearly pastors may be asked to participate by bringing greetings, a charge to the church, a word of prayer and a welcome into the local pastors' fellowship. The chairperson of the team usually speaks briefly, recounting the process and rejoicing in the cooperation received. See Chapter Sixteen for more            on              this              topic.

A reception after the service with simple refreshments is customary. It is always a nice touch when a large, attractively-decorated cake in the middle of a table welcomes the new family. A love gift is sometimes given to help with the costs of settling into a new home.

## CONCLUSION

The Lord will reward your hard efforts with a beautiful on-going relationship with your new shepherd. And may you marvel at the blessing of God upon your church! A great welcome is one way to assure    a    long    tenure    for    your    new    pastor.

## PASTORAL DISCOVERY TEAM- CHAPTER FIFTEEN *WORK IT OUT!*

Discuss and assign who will do the various follow-up mentioned in this chapter. Write down feedback and strategies for the main points of chapter fifteen.

1. _____

2. _____

3. _____

4. _____

5. _____

6. _____

List any other ways you will accomplish the steps in chapter fifteen for welcoming the pastor:

_____

_____

_____

_____

_____

What others needs and issues need to be considered at this point? _____

_____

Together, as a team, take time to thank the Lord for the opportunity of moving your pastor and welcoming him into his new home. Ask Him to give you a sense of satisfaction regarding the role you played at this juncture of your new pastor's family's life. Determine who will carry out this "plan of welcome." Execute the plan with precision.

## CHAPTER SIXTEEN
### Installation: Installing Your New Pastor

The big night (or morning) is finally here! It is time for your church to "officially" install (welcome) your new pastor. This is sure to be one of the highlights of your church's history! As with a wedding, you have only one chance to "pull this off," so plan and execute wisely and efficiently. You have already set the date and made the preparations. Here are some tips to make your pastor's installation a success.

**1. Who Should Be at the Installation Service?**

The first thing you have to do is decide who will be participating in the installation service. You will need the following positions filled to assure a great ceremony.

a. Speakers

You will need at least two speakers, though you may want to have more. You or your new pastor should invite ordained men who have impacted the life of your new pastor. These may be pastors, college and seminary professors, mentors, etc. Two of your speakers should each address one of the following:

- Charge to the Pastor

  One speaker will want to address the pastor with a timely and Scriptural message that will speak of his calling, responsibility, expectations, etc. This should be a sober, yet encouraging message.

- Charge to the People (Church)

  One of the remaining speakers should address the congregation. This message should speak of the congregation's responsibility in encouraging and supporting the pastor, as well as a reminder of its duty to follow the pastor's leading. It should be an upbeat and positive message.

- Other

  Other speakers may address such topics as the church or pastor deem appropriate and necessary.

b. Musicians

Most pastors will want music at their service. There are many hymns and popular songs that are appropriate for such an occasion, and only your creativity will limit you here. You will want to consider:

- Instrumentalists (piano, organ, praise band, etc.)

- Vocalists

- Choir

- Praise Team

- Other: _____

c. Deacons (or Elders)

The pastor will want to include the deacons (or elders), as they will be instrumental in his ministry and potential success. In some cases, they are the ones who called the pastor. This can be very meaningful to the church.

d. Family

You may want to include family members, at least in a "testimonial" role. A father or mother (or both parents), sibling, etc., can really add to the personable-ness of the service.

e. The Pastoral Discovery Team (PDT)

If at all possible, try to have the people (or a portion) who served on the PDT present at the actual installation. This will add to the official-ness of the meeting, and add credibility to the process. This is also a real joy for the PDT members.

f. Master of Ceremonies (MC)

Someone will need to lead the ceremony. This may be the pastor's guest, the chairman of board, or whomever the pastor or church deems appropriate.

g. Attendees

Of course, anyone and everyone who has a love for and interest in the pastor (all church members, his family, friends, etc.) should be officially invited (preferably by written invitation) to the ceremony.

h. Press Release

Consider sending a press release to the local newspaper inviting the general public. This may interest searching individuals who may continue their search at the church in the future.

i. Others: _____

## 2. When is the Service Scheduled?

There are two things to consider regarding the "when" of the installation service: 1) the date; and 2) the time. How soon after the arrival will you have the service? Is there adequate time to prepare? Do not let too much time go by. Be quick, but do it well! Will you have an AM or PM installation service? In almost all cases, a PM is preferable for a variety of reasons, but the choice is up to you. The main thing is to consider all the components of the service, and scrutinize the variables that will be affected by the time you choose.

## 3. Order of Installation Service

There are many elements of an installation service. The following is a partial list:

a. Music

- Congregational Music

- Special Music

b. Messages

- Charge to the Pastor

- Charge to the Congregation

c. Recognitions (Wife, Family, Mentors, etc.)

d. Prayer and Anointing (Laying on of Hands by Ordained Men or Elders)

e. Testimonies

f. Presentation of the Pastor

g. Presentation of the Certificate of Installation

h. Other: _____

## 4. Gifts to Be Given

It is quite appropriate to give the new pastor a gift. This can be a new Bible (preferably a genuine leather one, not bonded leather or other imitation), books, money, desk accessory, etc. Be creative. Unless it is a surprise, consult the pastor in advance. If you want to surprise him, consult his wife. This should be presented at or near the end of the service.

Also consider giving the pastor's wife a gift or other token of affection. Many churches even do this for the kids. The "sky is the limit!"

## 5. Other: _____

## CONCLUSION

If you will follow these guidelines, or some like them, you will enjoy a very exciting, organized, and well-executed installation service that will be a fond memory for your church and the pastor and his family for the rest of their lives.

**PASTORAL DISCOVERY TEAM- CHAPTER SIXTEEN *WORK IT OUT!***

Discuss and assign who will do the various follow-up mentioned in this chapter. Write down feedback and strategies for the main points of chapter sixteen.

1. _____

2. _____

3. _____

4. _____

5. _____

List any other ways you will accomplish the steps in chapter sixteen for the installation service:

_____

_____

_____

_____

_____

What others needs and issues need to be considered at this point? _____

_____

Together, as a team, take time to thank the Lord for the opportunity for "installing" your pastor and welcoming him into his new church home. Ask Him to give you a sense of satisfaction regarding the role you played at this juncture of your new pastor's family's life and the life of your church.

## CONCLUSION
## Implementation: Taking Care of Your New Pastor

Everyone desires that their pastor remains for a good long time and that their church has their best ministry years yet. One way to accomplish this is to "take good care of your pastor." I have written a booklet that will help you do just that. Feel free to contact me at or visit my website at www.GregoryKTyree.com to get a copy (or copies) of *Fifty Ways to Love Your Pastor*. (Note: This booklet has been revised and reprinted to reflect ministry needs in the 21st Century.)

Keep this present volume handy for the future, as you may someday (hopefully a long time away) need it again. In the meantime, enjoy your new pastor and his family, follow his leadership, and join in with what God is going to do in your church. Thanks for using this resource!

**Appendix One**
**THE "TEAM" INTERVIEW**

The spiritual qualifications of a pastor, listed in I Timothy 3 and Titus 1 must guide you in evaluating a man's fitness to be your candidate. Likewise, Ephesians 4; I Timothy 4; II Timothy 4; Hebrews 13 and I Peter 5 set forth some of the functions of a pastor. Study these Scriptures, and then interview a prospective pastor regarding some specific matters. The "TEAM" concept gives you an outline of four areas of interrogation . . .

T--TESTIMONY

- When and how did you come to faith in Christ?

- When and how did you sense a desire to become a pastor?

- Is there anything in our doctrinal statement that you question?

- What do you believe are the marks of a Bible-believing church with baptistic convictions?

E--EXPERIENCE

- What ministries have you had and with what results?

- What education or special seminars have you had and how has this training strengthened your ministry?

- What are some special lessons God has taught you that would be helpful for our church?

A--AIMS

- What is your vision for local church ministry?

- What is your view of small group ministry?

- What is your view of seeker-sensitive services?

- How do you plan to develop leaders in the church?

- What personal goals do you have for your life?

- How would you seek to relate to the boards in our church?

- What method of preaching would you use?

- How would you aim to implement organizational changes?

- What is your burden for ministry to youth and senior saints?

- What would be your emphasis on evangelism, missions and stewardship?

- What is your plan for visitation?

M--MATE (Directed to the wife)

- When and how did you come to know Christ? How do you maintain the priority of the family?

- How do you view your husband's ministry?

**Appendix Two**
**LETTER OF INQUIRY**

(Note: Be sure to adapt for your use and type personally. Do not use a form letter with blanks filled in.)

FIRST BAPTIST CHURCH
Pleasant Town, USA

July 15, 2004

Dear Pastor Nicename:

Your resume has been referred to us by a friend of our church as one who might be available for a new challenge.

Our church is located in a community of great opportunity in the western part of our state. Average Sunday morning attendance is 105, and our fine facilities have space for anticipated growth.

Are you interested at this time in exploring with us the possibility of pastoring our church? We realize that much prayer and much exchange of information are necessary in the process of determining God's will. We simply want to know if we may pursue the matter further with you.

Kindly let us know within two weeks of receipt of this letter if you are open to consider the possibility of becoming our pastor. We will then forward a packet of information and seek to become better acquainted.

Sincerely in Christ,


Mrs. Ima Asking

Secretary, Pastoral Discovery Team

**Appendix Three**
**REFERENCE FORM**

FIRST BAPTIST CHURCH
Pleasant Town, USA

July 15, 1996

YOUR NAME . . . _____ has been given as
one who knows Rev. John Nicename.

He is under consideration as a possible candidate for the pastorate of our church.
Credibility for God's service is a serious matter. Would you, therefore, comment
briefly on as many of the following areas as possible?

Your response will be accorded the highest confidentiality. Thank you for your
help and promptness. A self-addressed envelope is enclosed for your convenience.

Sincerely,


Mrs. Ima Asking
Secretary, Search Committee


1. His reputation . . .
2. His personality . . .
3. His preaching . . .
4. His past ministry . . .
5. His strengths . . .

6. Any cautions . . .
7. Leadership style . . .
8. His wife's helpfulness . . .
9. His children . . .
10. His activity with Baptists . . .

Relationship to the above man:

Additional comments:


Other names to contact if they will not to jeopardize the pastor's present ministry:


Signed: _____

Appendix Four
## TERMS OF CALL

FIRST BAPTIST CHURCH
Pleasant Town, USA
July 15, 1996

TERMS OF CALL

VOTE TO CALL . . .

Yes votes:_____;  No Votes:_____; Abstentions_____

TENURE . . .

The term of service is to continue indefinitely. Notification of termination is to be by thirty day notice and mutual agreement.

FINANCIAL PROVISIONS . . .

Annual cash salary- $ _____
Housing allowance (parsonage or private home)- _____
Social Security allowance- _____
Allowance for journals/education- _____
Automobile reimbursement- _____
Health insurance- _____
Disability insurance- _____
Retirement plan- _____
Other- _____

HOUSING ARRANGEMENTS . . .

Many churches are encouraging their pastors to purchase their own home. Sometimes churches assist with the down payment. A housing allowance is provided for the expenses of the home.

Other churches provide a parsonage with utilities and phone included. Repairs on parsonage should be cared for by the Board of Deacons/Trustees. The church should specify the responsibilities of the pastor for the lawn care and snow removal.

CHURCH CONFERENCES . . .

It is expected that the pastor attend the annual conference of the regional CB fellowship. Actual expenses of registration, travel, food and lodging to be paid by the church. If the pastor's wife is able to accompany him, her lodging and meals will be paid by the church. Time spent at CB conferences or church camping functions need not be deducted from vacation allowance.

TIME-OFF CONSIDERATIONS . . .

Four weeks of vacation with full salary will be granted within each twelve months. This time may be taken in two or more segments, if desired. Arrangements of time away and a schedule of suitable speakers are to be worked out with the leadership team.

At least one day off each week is encouraged, and sufficient other time to give quality attention to the needs of the pastor's family.

Two Sundays for ministry elsewhere will be granted with the pastor responsible for personally reimbursing his pulpit replacements.

Time off for medical needs will be granted up to thirty days within a calendar year. More time needed than that will be reviewed by the church leadership.

MOVING ARRANGEMENTS . . .

Trucking costs and family travel expenses (including lodging and meals) will be prepaid or reimbursed by the church in accordance with arrangements made with the Search Committee.

The above terms have been authorized by the congregation along with the invitation for you to become pastor. Please sign and return one copy of these arrangements, indicating your agreement. Please indicate, too, the date of your arrival in the parsonage and the first Sunday you expect to be in the pulpit.

Sincerely in Christ,
Mrs. Ima Asking
Secretary, Pastoral Discovery Team

I understand the above terms and agree to them,

(Signed)_____

(Date)_____

**Appendix Five**
**SAMPLE LETTER OF CALL**

Dear Mr. Peterson:

It is my pleasure to inform you that, by vote of our congregation on Wednesday, February 18, 2013, the First Baptist Church extends to you a unanimous call to become its pastor. The enthusiastic spirit of our people was a joy to us, as we hope it will be to you.

The terms of the call as ratified by the church tonight are as follows:
The church agrees:

(In dollars, list policies, remuneration income, expenses, and benefits.)

You, as pastor-elect, agree:

1. To accept the pastoral leadership of the First Baptist Church beginning your ministry on April 1, 2013.
2. To assume payments for your participation as a self-employed person in Social Security (and if it is agreed that he will pay a percentage of his retirement plan, that should also be so stated).
3. To work to the best of your ability within the framework of the Church and Association Statement of Faith and with the mission our denomination.
4. To the provision in the By-Laws of the First Baptist Church, whereby pastoral relationship may be terminated by either pastor or church upon giving three months' notice or by such notice as may be mutually agreed upon by both parties.

We have endeavored to outline as carefully and completely as possible, for your assurance and that of the church, the arrangements implicit in this call, and we will appreciate having your written acceptance at the earliest possible date.

May God bless you.

By order of the church, Signed:

_____
(Chairman of the church)

_____
(Church Clerk)

_____
(Chairman of the Pastoral Discovery Team

**Appendix Six**
**SAMPLE PRAYER AND COMMITMENT CARD**

PRAYER PLEDGE CARD

---

### *PRAYER PLEDGE CARD*

I, _____, pledge to pray

daily for God's direction for our church, and his

wisdom for our calling committee during the selection

of our new pastor.

*Please memorize James 1: 5 and 6*

Our Pastoral Discovery Team members are:

| | |
|---|---|
| John Smith | Robert Brown |
| James Jones | Kay Olson |
| Faith Johnson | Ed Larson |

---

**Appendix Seven**
**INSTALLATION SERVICE**

*Plan this in consultation with your new pastor to be held as soon after his arrival as convenient. Someone other than the pastor should emcee it--perhaps the Search Committee chairperson.*

- Prelude

- Hymn

- Invocation (Guest pastor)

- Scripture reading (Guest pastor)

- Welcome to Pastor and Family (Chairman, Board of Elders/Deacons)

- Presentations (A corsage could be presented to the pastor's wife. If a love gift has been collected, it can be presented here.)

- Special Music

- Welcome to [Denomination] (Representative of the regional or local association.)

- Installation Message

- Charge to the church (Guest speaker)

- Charge to the pastor (Guest speaker)

- Response by the Pastor (A few words of appreciation and challenge.)

- Closing hymn

- Benediction (Guest pastor or new pastor)

- Postlude

*Guests are invited to a reception in the fellowship hall after the service.*

(Information about the new pastor may be included on the facing page of the special bulletin for this occasion. Also, a "thank you" for the work of the Search committee is in order.)

**Appendix Eight**
## PASTORAL DISCOVERY TEAM (PDT) PROCEDURE CHECKLIST

➢ ORGANIZING

  ❑ PDT tasks determined
  ❑ Meeting times established
  ❑ PDT costs arranged
  ❑ Interim pulpit arrangements made

➢ DATA-GATHERING

  ❑ Poll conducted
  ❑ Church Information Form returned to association
  ❑ Screening guidelines adopted
  ❑ Church purpose clarified
  ❑ Financial package projected
  ❑ Vacation to be offered

➢ SECURING NAMES

  ❑ Schools contacted
  ❑ Resume form duplicated
  ❑ Decide content of Letter in Inquiry
  ❑ Provide safe filing and handling systems

➢ SELECTING CANDIDATE

  ❑ List phone questions for prospects
  ❑ Prepare personal interview items
  ❑ Compile information packet
  ❑ Arrange for playing cassettes
  ❑ Duplicate reference form
  ❑ Plan travel and visit procedures
  ❑ Choose candidate

➢ PRESENTING CANDIDATE

  ❑ Schedule date and details
  ❑ Reserve accommodations
  ❑ Publicize schedule
  ❑ Arrange reimbursement
  ❑ Review weekend

➢ EXTENDING THE CALL

- ❏ Plan business session
- ❏ Consult constitution for details
- ❏ Prepare motion and ballots
- ❏ Notify candidate of vote
- ❏ Mail terms of call
- ❏ Announce his decision

➢ WELCOMING CANDIDATE

- ❏ Make moving arrangements
- ❏ Prepare parsonage
- ❏ Hold food shower
- ❏ Arrange arrival help
- ❏ Plan                                              installation

Appendix Nine
## THE INTERIM: PULPIT SUPPLY OR INTERIM PASTOR
Excerpt from *Procedures in Calling a Pastor* by Emmett V. Johnson

### Changing Pulpit Supply

Different guest speakers are asked to come each Sunday. This is the least expensive but also the least desirable. The church generally gets a hodgepodge of good sermons—but sometimes two speakers may use the same text! The system gives an air of uncertainty to the congregations, especially to those two who are not members. Further, it is a frustrating task for the vice-chairman or coordinator of the system. Mix-ups occur. Sometimes two men show up on the same Sunday, or no one shows, or he comes at the wrong hour. The system is only tolerable.

### Constant Pulpit Supply or Interim Preacher

One man is asked to fill the pulpit only. The weakness of such a situation (as in the first) is apparent: the other areas of ministry suffer. If a church is forced to go the route of pulpit supply, as is the case with many smaller town and country churches, the responsibility of calling and counseling must be assumed by the deacons. Time is always a problem but we can cite cases where laymen have taken the responsibility and the ministry was prospered.

### Part-Time Interim Pastor

Usually this person serves the church several days a week and commutes to the church. He does all the preaching, conducts wedding and funeral services, does visitation and is available for counseling. His time is limited but the people know that he is available in time of need.

### Full-Time Interim Pastor

A retired minister, denominational personnel, missionaries on furlough and seminary students are people who can be capable interim pastors of skill and ability, as well as being able to give time to such a ministry. This is generally viewed as the ideal situation. The work moves forward and even increases in many instances. For a large church it is a must. For any church which recognizes that there will be a sizeable interim period, the interim pastor ---part or full time— seems to be the best route.

Lyle Schaller delineates six types of parish situations in which the concept of an interim pastor merits serious consideration.

1. When the pastor who has served his congregation for over fifteen years dies or retires. An interim of six months to two years is needed. "In approximately four out of five of such

parishes, regardless of whether the pastor dies or retires after his fifteen or twenty or thirty or forty years there, the next minister is an interim pastor."

2. The second type of parish where an interim pastorate may be appropriate is closely related to the first. " It is the church whose pastor, after fifteen or twenty years' service, moves on to another parish or to some non-parish position. His successor faces more favorable odds than the first type, but, in a majority of the cases studied, the next minister also is an interim pastor--- though frequently he does not realize it until several years later."

3. Where there has been a strong authoritarian type of leadership (a type now in sharp decline in term of popularity!), in order for the new style of collaborative leadership with a broad base of participation to come into being, it seems best that an interim pastor follow such a strong authoritative leader

4. Following a young pastor who has died

5. Where there has been major internal disturbance in the church --- the church has polarized or gone downhill or the pastor asked to leave by reason of heresy, morals or incompetence.

6. Where there is a major change coming, an interim pastor may be needed to bridge the two eras, e.g., in the white congregation in a community into which an increasing number of blacks or Spanish-speaking persons are moving, or in the rural church which finds itself now engulfed by the city.

The interim pastor, who has no future with the church, comes only to serve the Lord Jesus Christ; usually a man of maturity, he can be used by God to bridge many gaps in order for the permanent pastor to come into a long, happy, fruitful pastorate.

The interim pastor should be carefully chosen. It is his task to build up. Generally speaking, he should not be a part of the pastoral selection process nor should he attend the meetings of the pulpit committee.

## ABOUT THE AUTHOR

Dr. Greg Tyree, PhD, is founding Pastor of GracePointe Baptist Church in Madison Heights, Virginia, where he has served a dynamic congregation since 2005. He has also pastored in New Jersey and Pennsylvania. Greg is the author of several books, including: *My Own Life Focus; My Own Life Map; My Own Life Time; Understanding Your Personality; Discovering Your Spiritual Gifts;* and *How to Lead Someone to Christ.* He has also written field manuals, including *Helping Your Church Discover Its Next Pastor,* and other useful resources and assessment tools that contribute to organizational, personal, and church health and growth. As a coach, he has developed several unique tools for life-enrichment, including *My-Own-Life-Focus*™ and *The FORWARD Coaching Model*™. He is available for a limited number of conferences and seminars. Greg has been married to the love of his life, Lois, since 1983. They have two beautiful children, Lauren and Stephen.

For copies of resources, or to schedule coaching, seminars, conferences, or consultations, contact Greg at:

112 Center Street
568 Winesap Road
Madison Heights, VA 24572
GregoryKTyree@cs.com
www.GregryKTyree.com

# Also by Greg Tyree

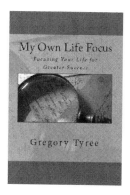

Most people start out their adult lives with clarity of purpose and a sincere mission and vision for their future. In short, they set out to change the world. But something happens along the way. Life-focusing can be the one thing that can change all that. By stepping back and looking at our life anew, we can literally get back that drive and vision of our youth, and make a real impact for good. Contentment, a sense of significance, and true joy can be ours if we are willing to do the hard work of life-focusing. That's where this book, *My Own Life Focus*, comes in.

Starting where *My Own Life Focus* left off, *My Own Life Map* is an eight-step personal strategic planning model that helps you map out your life to accomplish your life-purpose and focus discovered through the life-focusing process. It is one thing to know that you want to go from New York to San Francisco, but is quite another to know how to get there. *My Own Life Map* helps you find your destination. While this book is a stand-alone volume, it works best when followed by the processes developed in *My Own Life Focus*.

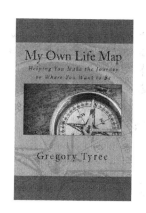

The final book in the *My Own Life Series, My Own Life Time* is also the most practical. While the first two volumes, *My Own Life Focus* and *My Own Life Map* dealt with the "big picture" issues of discovering your purpose and mapping out your life for success, *My Own Life Time* is "where the rubber meets the road," giving you tools and ideas to help you in your day-to-day time and life-management. While the book focuses on those in professional careers, it is helpful to anyone that desires to manage their life better.

Find these titles at Amazon.com or at the author's site, www.GregoryKTyree.com

Made in the USA
Middletown, DE
22 May 2016